VOGUE® KNITTING

# STITCHIONARY™ 3

The Ultimate Stitch Dictionary from the Editors of Vogue® Knitting Magazine

volume three
color knitting

VOGUE® KNITTING

# STITCHIONARY™ 3

The Ultimate Stitch Dictionary from the Editors of Vogue® Knitting Magazine

volume three
color knitting

Sixth&Spring Books
233 Spring Street
New York, New York 10013

Editorial Director
Trisha Malcolm

Book Editor
Carla Scott

Art Director
Chi Ling Moy

Graphic Designer
Sheena T. Paul

Project Coordinator
Eve Ng

Instructions Editors
Lisa Buccellato
Louisa Cameron-Smith

Technical Illustrations
Uli Mönch
Frances Soohoo

Yarn Editor
Tanis Gray

Associate Editor
Erin Walsh

Book Division Manager
Erica Smith

Production Manager
David Joinnides

President and Publisher, Sixth&Spring Books
Art Joinnides

1  3  5  7  9  10  8  6  4  2
Manufactured in China

Library of Congress Control Number: 2006924842
ISBN: 1-933027-02-9
ISBN-13: 978-1-933027-02-9

Photo Credits:
Jack Deutsch (Front cover, back cover, and all swatches)
Paul Amato (pp. 9, 33, 75, 115)
Jim Jordan (p. 151)

# contents

We dedicate this book to all the staff at SoHo Publishing, whose hard work, dedication and expertise make the *Stitchionary* series a resounding and continuing success!

It is hard to imagine how quickly we completed the first two volumes of the *Vogue Knitting Stitchionary*—Volume One (Knit & Purl) and Volume Two (Cables)—and that we now have a new volume on color knitting. It continues to amaze me that there is so much one can create with the simple art of knitting.

We devised an individual color palette for each of the first two volumes, but this book is exclusively about color. For that reason, we needed more than just a single color palette. Choosing from all the colors available was no easy task! Working with our art director, Chi Ling Moy (a knitter herself), everything came together. For the Slip Stitch chapter, we settled on oranges and greens; for

Adding Textures, blues and ecru; for two-color, a more basic color palette: ecru, black, yellow, red and grey. Then we got to the Fair Isle/Multicolor and Intarsia/Motifs chapters, in which each swatch has its own array of colors. In these instances, we tried to match the color combinations from the original designs that appeared in *Vogue Knitting*. As this wasn't always feasible, we had to think outside of the box and choose what we felt were suitable substitutes.

This brings me to an issue that has been around since I started in the industry: When we design garments for our magazine, we work with the colors of the season. However, this does not necessarily mean that you must use the color (or colors) that we have chosen. Perhaps orange is the color for autumn, but it's the wrong color for your skin tone. In that case, you could choose, say, a beautiful blue instead.

In keeping with the first two volumes, we challenge you to be creative and dream up your own designs. Patterns that utilize two or more colors are a little more difficult than single-color knitting, so you might want to start by drawing your motifs on graph paper with colored pencils. Or look at a favorite garment or piece of fabric to see what colors go well together. If you follow your instincts and your individual taste, the sky is the limit!

Carla Scott

*ooh las vegas p. 63*

# how to use this book

The *Vogue Knitting Stitchionary, Volume Three: Color Knitting* is made up of five chapters: Two Color, Fair Isle/Multicolor, Intarsia/Motifs, Adding Texture, and Slip Stitch. For the most part, within each chapter, the stitches are presented in order of difficulty from easiest to hardest.

We charted all but a few of the patterns in this book. The colors used in the charts are as close as possible to the colors in the swatch. When two or more colors were too similar, we exaggerated one of them to help you distinguish them. Also, where black was used, the chart shows grey, making it easier to read.

Unless otherwise stated, the swatches were worked in stockinette stitch (knit on the right-side rows and purled on the wrong-side rows). Selvage stitches (usually worked in garter stitch) were sometimes added along the sides of the swatch to keep the edges from curling too much. These extra stitches and rows were not included in the written or charted instructions.

Depending on size, some swatches show only one repeat, while others show several repeats.

The Two-Color, Intarsia/Motifs and Fair Isle/Multicolor chapters show only charts, no written instructions—the patterns are very visual and self-explanatory. If there is a single motif, the chart shows only the motif, whereas the swatch may have added stitches and rows in the background color.

In the Adding Texture and Slip Stitch chapters, the swatches incorporate different stitches as well as color. The charts are made in color with the symbols included for the various stitches, such as cable crosses, purl stitches, or slip stitches. In every case, these charts are accompanied by a set of written instructions.

The Slip Stitch chapter is the most challenging of all the chapters. The charts show the working color used in each row, and the slipped stitches are represented by symbols. Many of the patterns in this chapter are best worked on double-pointed needles or circular needles. When you are working with several colors and the stripes are odd-numbered, you may not always have the color you want at the correct end of the needle to work the next stripe. In this instance, if working with double-pointed needles or circulars, you can simply slide the stitches to the end of the needle where your next color is hanging. Therefore, you may be working two right-side (or wrong-side) rows together.

As always, we encourage you to use your imagination and creativity. Do not be afraid to change the color scheme from what we have presented. In more complex patterns with three or more colors, we have coded the colors with MC (main color for where there is a distinct background color), A, B, C, and so on. This will facilitate the substitution of colors. Just make a new color key with a snip of each of your own colors, and place the corresponding letter next to it—that way, when you are reading the written pattern or chart, you can easily slot in your color choices.

two-color

# 1 snow berries

4

1

2-st rep

**Color Key**

□ white

■ red

# 2 blue bias

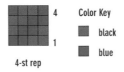

4

1

4-st rep

**Color Key**

■ black

■ blue

# 3 jailbird

# 4 office space

2
1

**4-st rep**

**Color Key**

☐ white

■ black

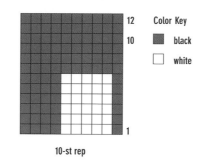

12

10

1

**10-st rep**

**Color Key**

■ black

☐ white

# 5 poseidon

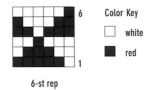

6

1

**6-st rep**

Color Key

☐ white

■ red

# 6 checkered past

8

1

**8-st rep**

Color Key

■ black

■ red

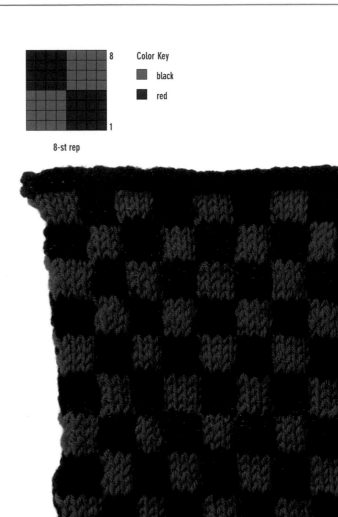

5

6

**Color Key**

yellow

blue

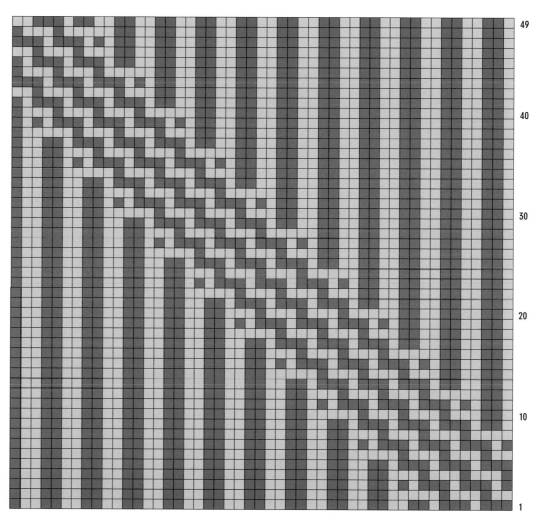

continue to shift pattern as established to desired length

49

40

30

20

10

1

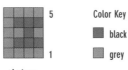

5

1

**4-st rep**

**Color Key**

black

grey

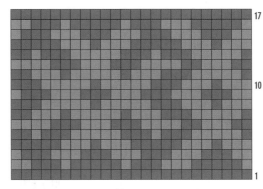

17

10

1

**24-st rep**

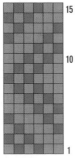

15

10

1

**6-st rep**

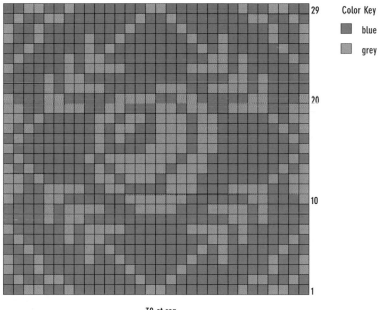

Color Key

■ blue

■ grey

30-st rep

# 10 tracks

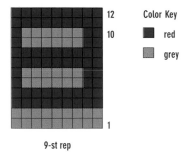

| | | 12 |
| | | 10 |
| | | 1 |

9-st rep

**Color Key**

■ red

■ grey

# 11 floating blocks

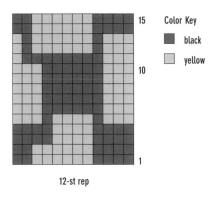

| | | 15 |
| | | 10 |
| | | 1 |

12-st rep

**Color Key**

■ black

■ yellow

**10**

**11**

## 12 houndstooth

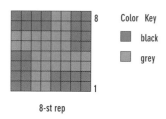

8

1

8-st rep

Color Key

■ black
■ grey

## 13 modern houndstooth

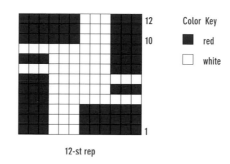

12

10

1

12-st rep

Color Key

■ red
□ white

12

13

## 14 modified houndstooth

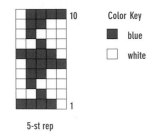

10

1

**5-st rep**

**Color Key**

■ blue

□ white

## 15 multi-tartan

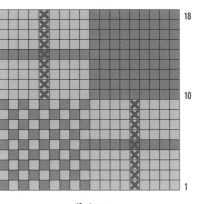

18

10

1

**18-st rep**

**Color Key**

■ yellow

■ black

✖ duplicate st in black

14

15

## 16 tanagrams

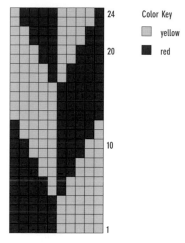

Color Key

- ▢ yellow
- ■ red

10-st rep

## 17 chesapeake

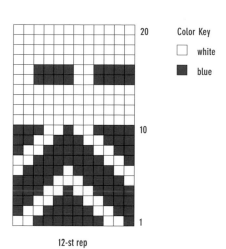

Color Key

- ▢ white
- ■ blue

12-st rep

16

17

Color Key

■ black

□ white

24-st rep

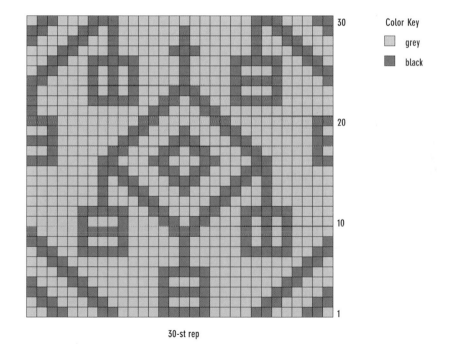

**Color Key**

□ grey

■ black

30-st rep

## 20 crimson and clover

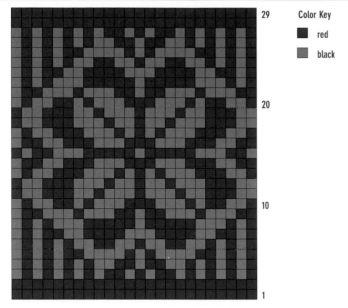

**Color Key**
- ■ red
- ■ black

24-st rep

## 21 damask

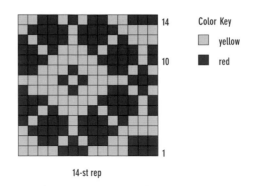

**Color Key**
- ☐ yellow
- ■ red

14-st rep

**Color Key**

☐ white

■ blue

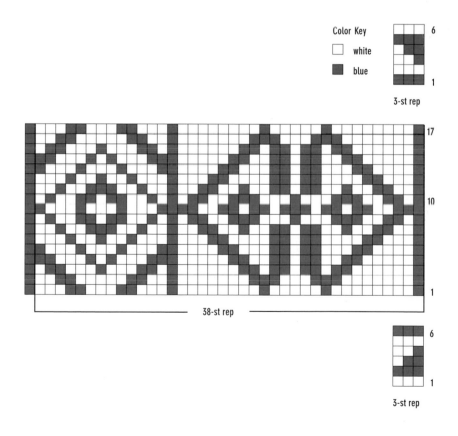

38-st rep

3-st rep

# 23 wallpaper

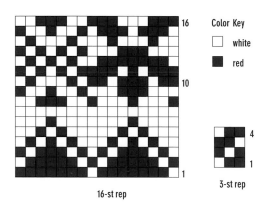

**Color Key**

☐ white

■ red

16-st rep

3-st rep

# 24 target

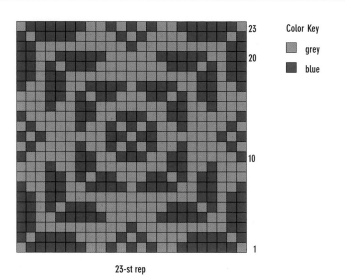

**Color Key**

■ grey

■ blue

23-st rep

23

24

## 25 patio

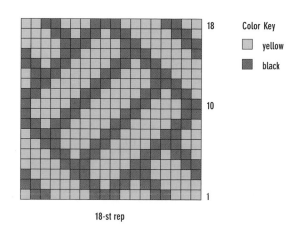

18-st rep

Color Key

■ yellow
■ black

## 26 chain link fence

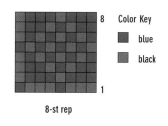

8-st rep

Color Key

■ blue
■ black

25

26

Color Key
☐ white
■ red

21 sts

21 sts

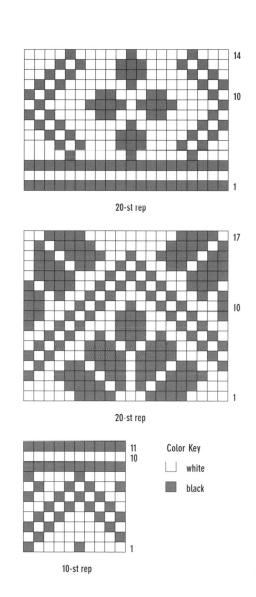

20-st rep

20-st rep

11
10

**Color Key**

☐ white

■ black

10-st rep

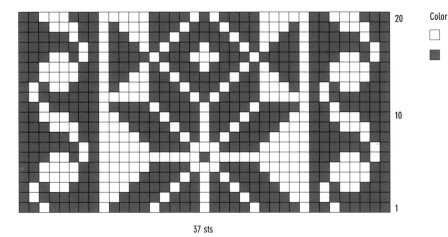

Color Key

☐ white

■ blue

37 sts

# two-color

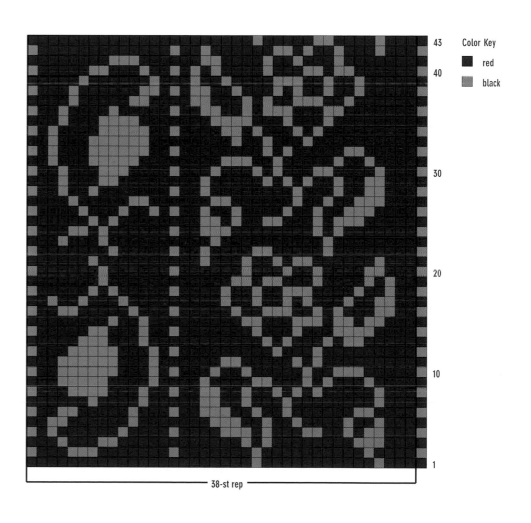

43

40

30

20

10

1

Color Key

■ red

■ black

38-st rep

30

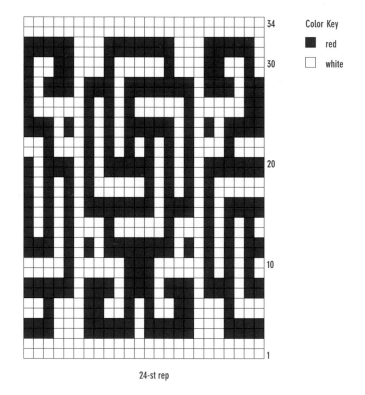

Color Key

■ red

☐ white

24-st rep

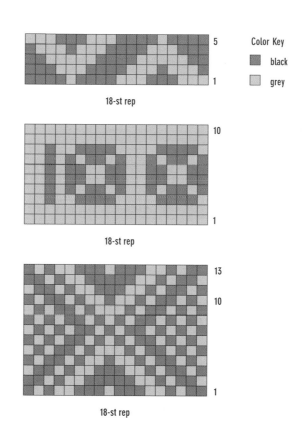

Color Key

█ black

░ grey

18-st rep

18-st rep

18-st rep

**Color Key**

- grey
- black
- — P on RS, K on WS

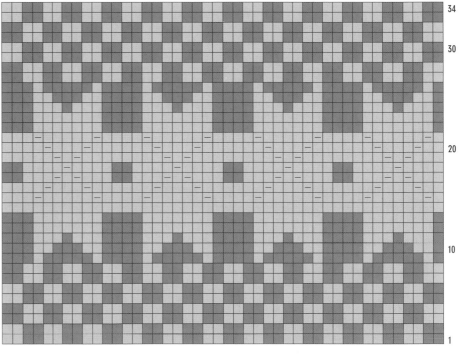

44-st rep

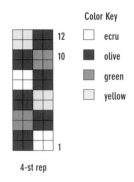

Color Key

☐ ecru

■ olive

■ green

☐ yellow

4-st rep

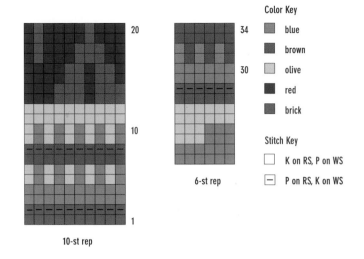

Color Key

■ blue

■ brown

■ olive

■ red

■ brick

Stitch Key

☐ K on RS, P on WS

⊟ P on RS, K on WS

6-st rep

10-st rep

34

35

# fair isle/multicolor

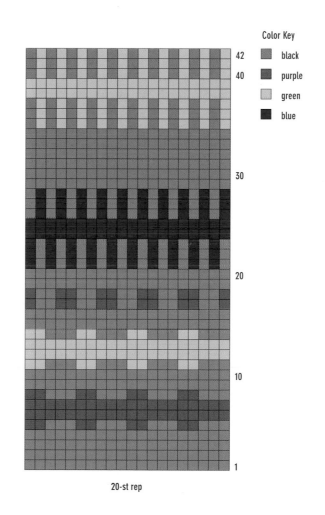

**Color Key**

- black
- purple
- green
- blue

20-st rep

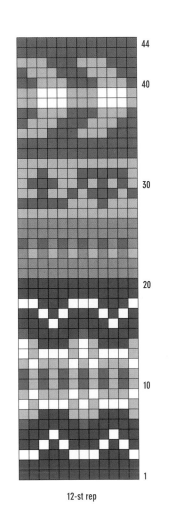

**Color Key**

☐ ecru
■ olive
■ blue
■ lime
■ sage
■ yellow
■ teal

44

40

30

20

10

1

**12-st rep**

# fair isle/multicolor

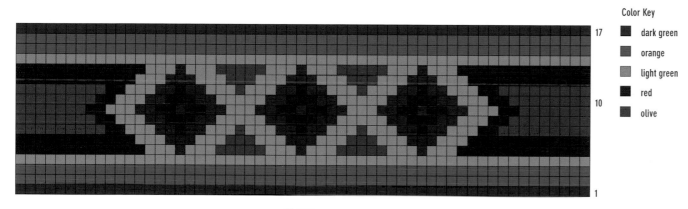

**Color Key**

■ dark green
■ orange
■ light green
■ red
■ olive

17

10

1

57-st rep

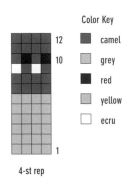

Color Key

| | |
|---|---|
| ■ | camel |
| ▨ | grey |
| ■ | red |
| ▨ | yellow |
| □ | ecru |

4-st rep

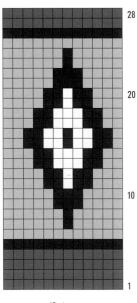

12-st rep

# fair isle/multicolor

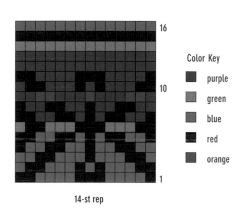

14-st rep

**Color Key**

■ purple
■ green
■ blue
■ red
■ orange

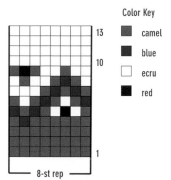

8-st rep

**Color Key**

■ camel
■ blue
□ ecru
■ red

**40**

**41**

Color Key

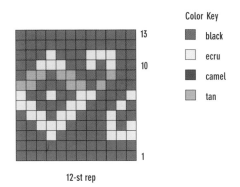

| | |
|---|---|
| ■ | black |
| ☐ | ecru |
| ■ | camel |
| ■ | tan |

12-st rep

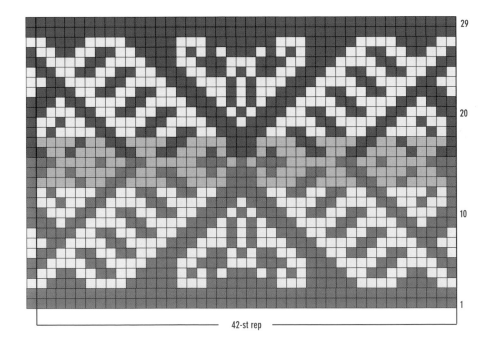

42-st rep

# fair isle/multicolor

**Color Key**

- green
- brown
- red
- purple
- lime
- blue
- yellow
- pink
- grape

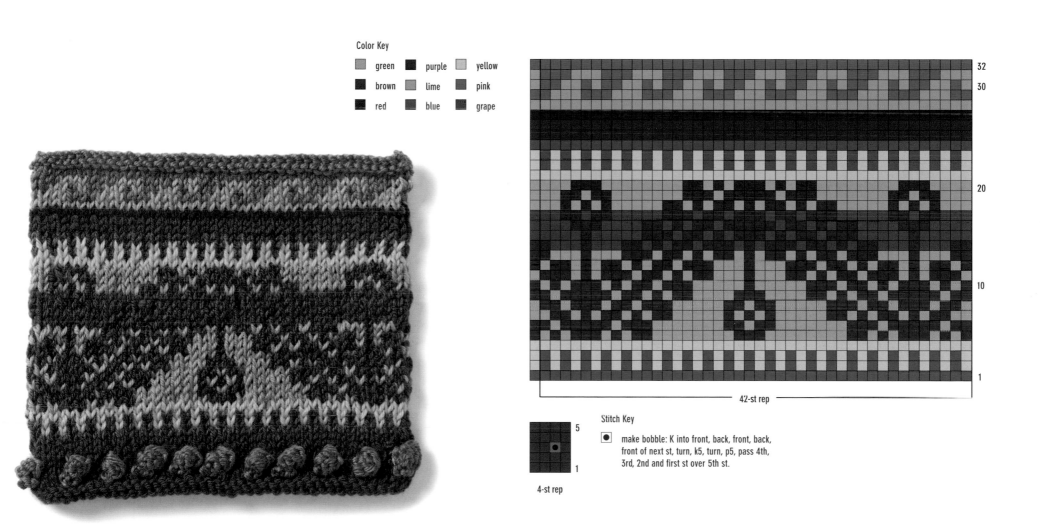

42-st rep

32
30
20
10
1

**Stitch Key**

⦿ make bobble: K into front, back, front, back, front of next st, turn, k5, turn, p5, pass 4th, 3rd, 2nd and first st over 5th st.

5

1

4-st rep

43

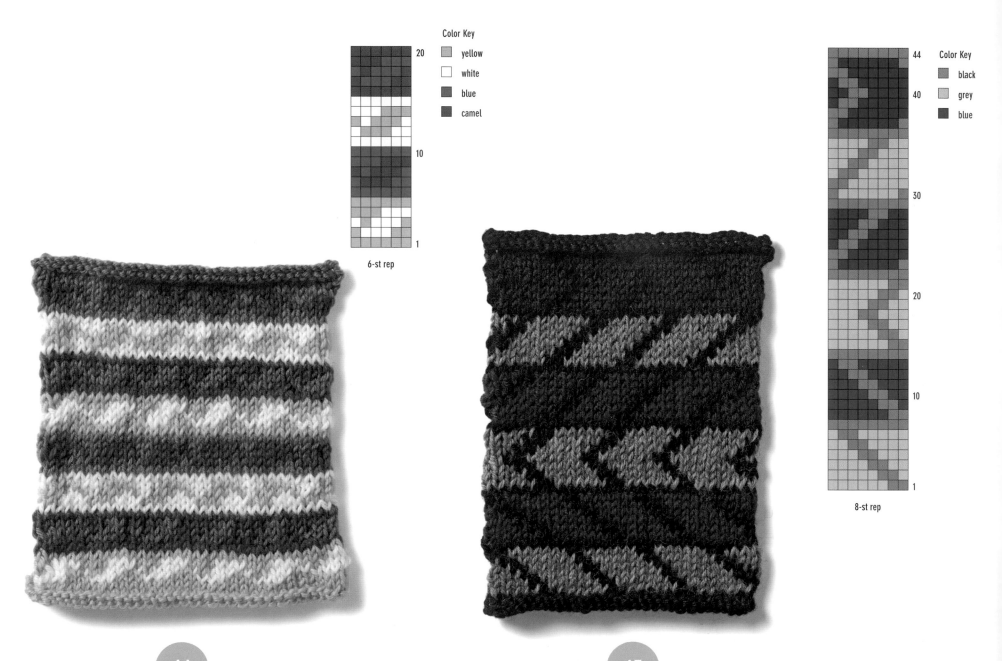

**Color Key**

| | |
|---|---|
| yellow | |
| white | |
| blue | |
| camel | |

6-st rep

**Color Key**

| | |
|---|---|
| black | |
| grey | |
| blue | |

8-st rep

44

45

# fair isle/multicolor

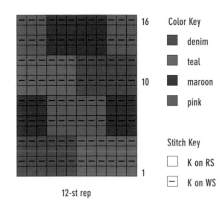

**Color Key**

■ denim

■ teal

■ maroon

■ pink

**Stitch Key**

☐ K on RS

⊟ K on WS

12-st rep

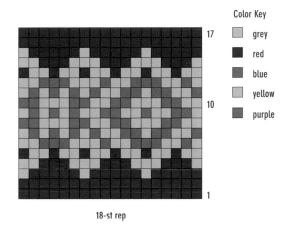

17

10

1

**Color Key**

☐ grey

■ red

■ blue

☐ yellow

■ purple

18-st rep

46

47

Color Key

■ brown
■ grey
□ ecru
■ blue
■ red
■ olive
■ brick

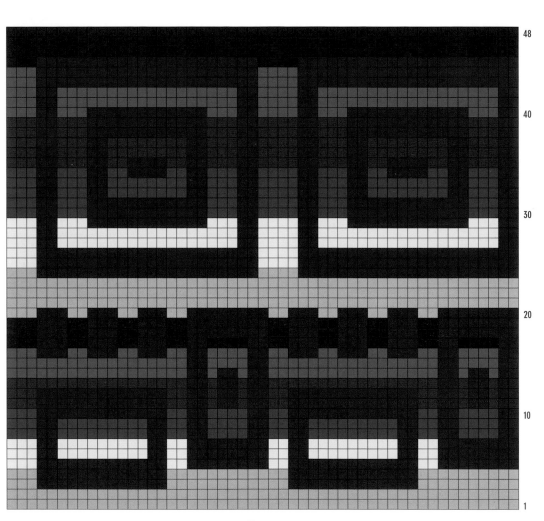

51-st rep

48

# fair isle/multicolor

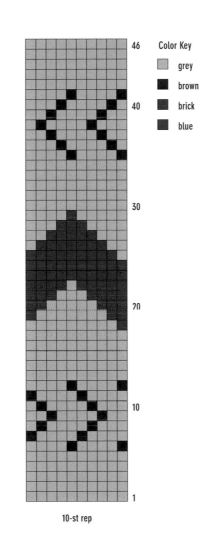

Color Key

- grey
- brown
- brick
- blue

10-st rep

Color Key

orange
red
pink
yellow

40-st rep

# fair isle/multicolor

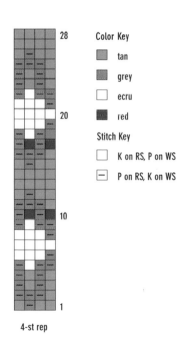

**Color Key**

- tan
- grey
- ecru
- red

**Stitch Key**

- ☐ K on RS, P on WS
- ⊟ P on RS, K on WS

4-st rep

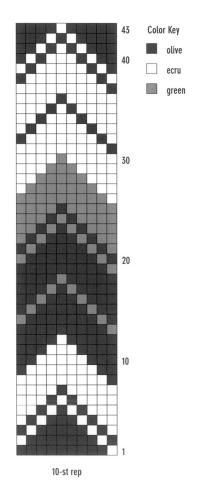

Color Key

■ olive

□ ecru

■ green

10-st rep

# fair isle/multicolor

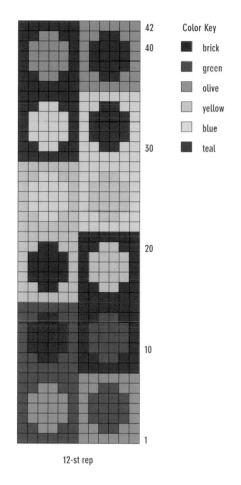

Color Key

■ brick
■ green
■ olive
■ yellow
□ blue
■ teal

12-st rep

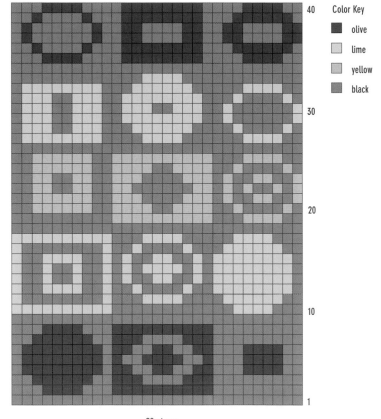

Color Key

■ olive
□ lime
□ yellow
■ black

40

30

20

10

1

29-st rep

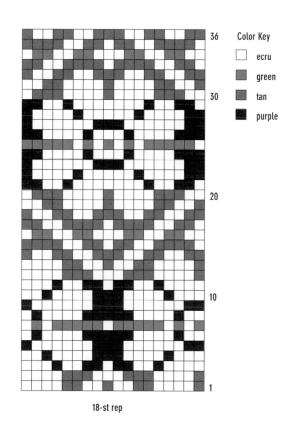

Color Key

☐ ecru

■ green

■ tan

■ purple

36

30

20

10

1

18-st rep

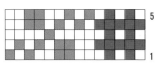

14-st rep

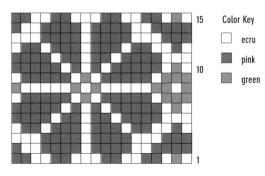

Color Key

▢ ecru

■ pink

■ green

18-st rep

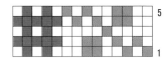

14-st rep

# fair isle/multicolor

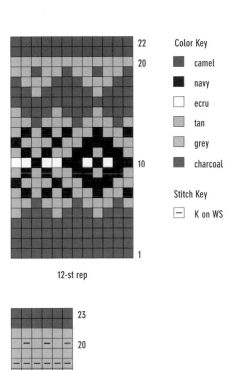

**Color Key**

- ■ camel
- ■ navy
- □ ecru
- ■ tan
- ■ grey
- ■ charcoal

**Stitch Key**

- ─ K on WS

12-st rep

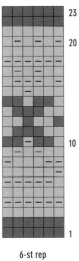

6-st rep

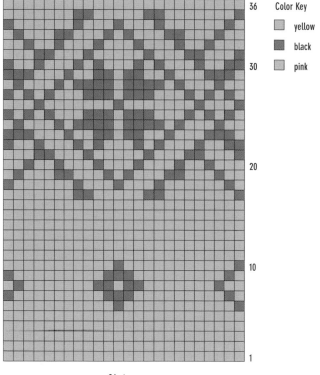

Color Key

- yellow
- black
- pink

**24-st rep**

# fair isle/multicolor

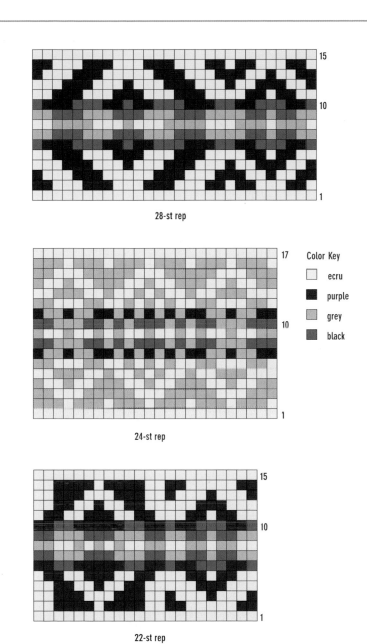

28-st rep

**Color Key**

| | |
|---|---|
| ☐ | ecru |
| ■ | purple |
| ■ | grey |
| ■ | black |

24-st rep

22-st rep

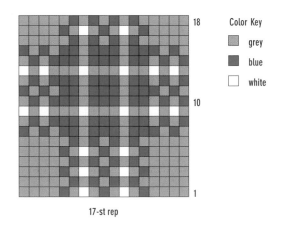

**Color Key**

grey

blue

white

18

10

1

17-st rep

# fair isle/multicolor

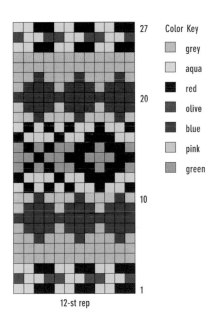

**Color Key**

- grey
- aqua
- red
- olive
- blue
- pink
- green

27
20
10
1

12-st rep

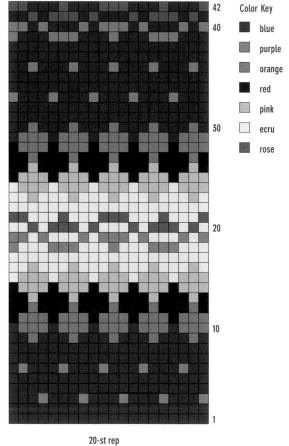

Color Key

- blue
- purple
- orange
- red
- pink
- ecru
- rose

20-st rep

# fair isle/multicolor

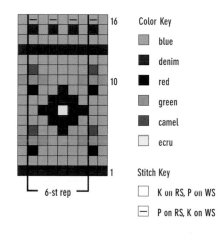

16

**Color Key**

- blue
- denim
- red
- green
- camel
- ecru

**Stitch Key**

- ☐ K on RS, P on WS
- ─ P on RS, K on WS

10

1

├─ 6-st rep ─┤

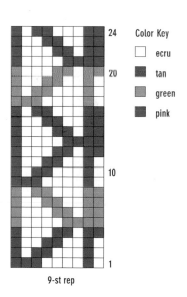

24

**Color Key**

- ☐ ecru
- ■ tan
- ■ green
- ■ pink

20

10

1

9-st rep

63

64

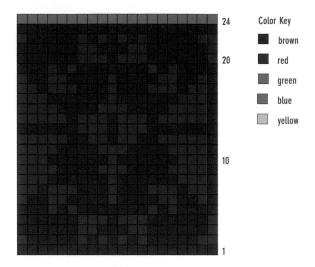

Color Key

brown

red

green

blue

yellow

24

20

10

1

20-st rep

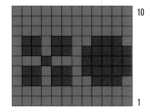

10

1

12-st rep

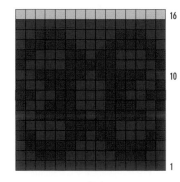

16

10

1

15-st rep

# fair isle/multicolor

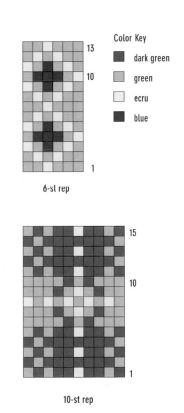

**Color Key**

- ■ dark green
- ■ green
- □ ecru
- ■ blue

6-st rep

10-st rep

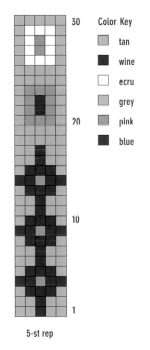

**Color Key**

- ■ tan
- ■ wine
- □ ecru
- ■ grey
- ■ pink
- ■ blue

5-st rep

66

67

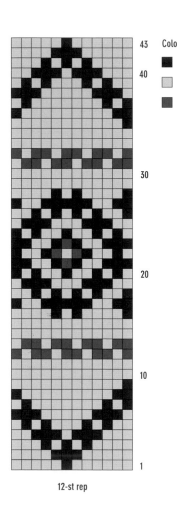

43

40

30

20

10

1

Color Key

■ brown

▢ grey

■ blue

12-st rep

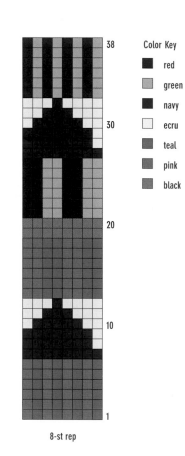

38

30

20

10

1

Color Key

■ red

■ green

■ navy

□ ecru

■ teal

■ pink

■ black

8-st rep

68

69

# fair isle/multicolor

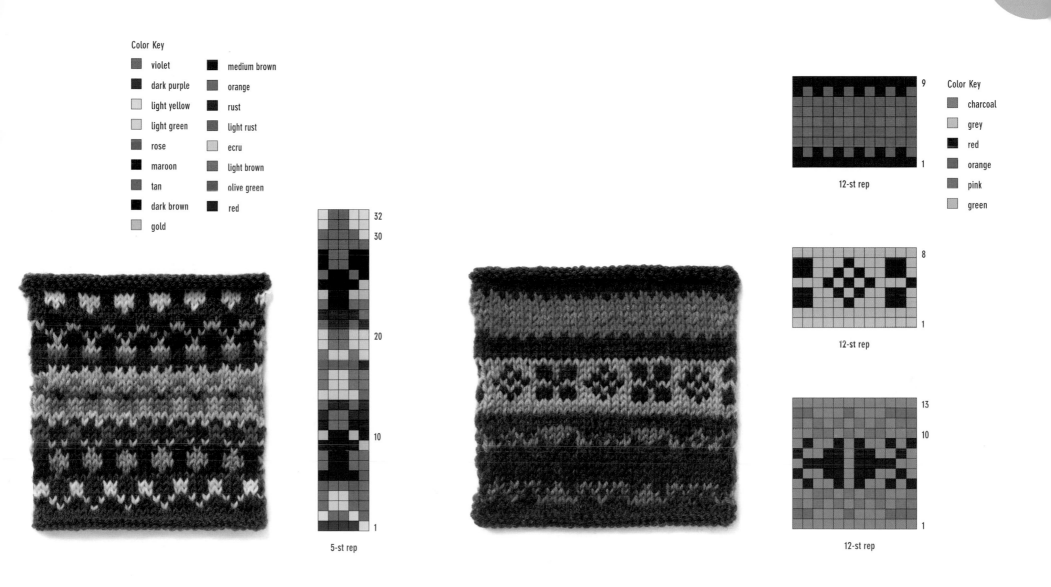

Color Key

| | | | |
|---|---|---|---|
| ■ | violet | ■ | medium brown |
| ■ | dark purple | ■ | orange |
| ☐ | light yellow | ■ | rust |
| ☐ | light green | ■ | light rust |
| ■ | rose | ☐ | ecru |
| ■ | maroon | ■ | light brown |
| ■ | tan | ■ | olive green |
| ■ | dark brown | ■ | red |
| ■ | gold | | |

5-st rep

Color Key

| | |
|---|---|
| ■ | charcoal |
| ☐ | grey |
| ■ | red |
| ■ | orange |
| ■ | pink |
| ☐ | green |

12-st rep

12-st rep

12-st rep

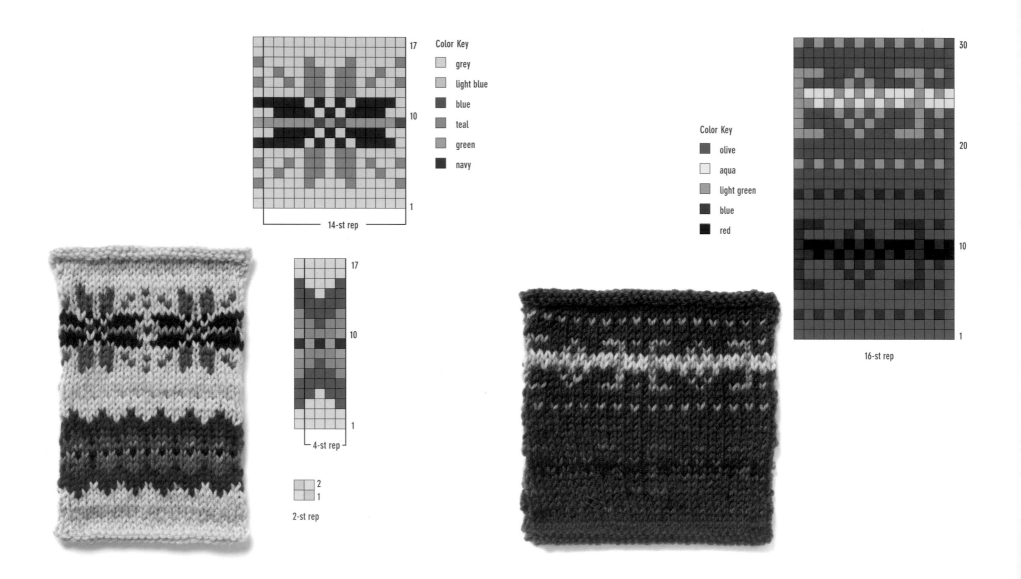

Color Key
- grey
- light blue
- blue
- teal
- green
- navy

14-st rep

17

10

1

17

10

1

4-st rep

2
1

2-st rep

Color Key
- olive
- aqua
- light green
- blue
- red

30

20

10

1

16-st rep

72

73

# fair isle/multicolor

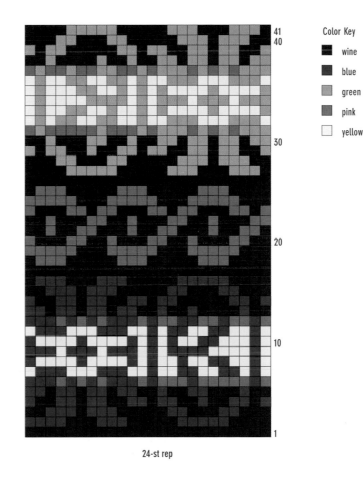

**Color Key**

- ■ wine
- ■ blue
- ■ green
- ■ pink
- □ yellow

41
40

30

20

10

1

24-st rep

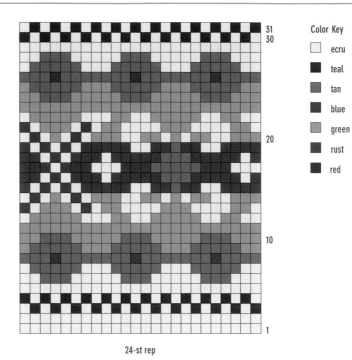

24-st rep

Color Key

| | |
|---|---|
| ☐ | ecru |
| ■ | teal |
| ■ | tan |
| ■ | blue |
| ■ | green |
| ■ | rust |
| ■ | red |

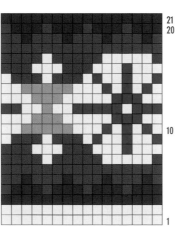

16-st rep

75

# fair isle/multicolor

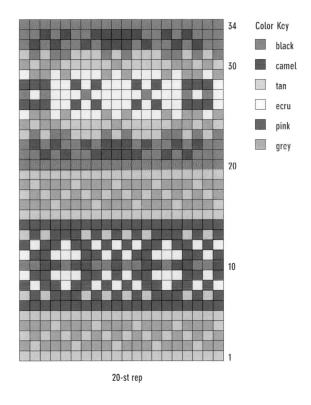

34

30

20

10

1

Color Key

■ black

■ camel

□ tan

□ ecru

■ pink

■ grey

**20-st rep**

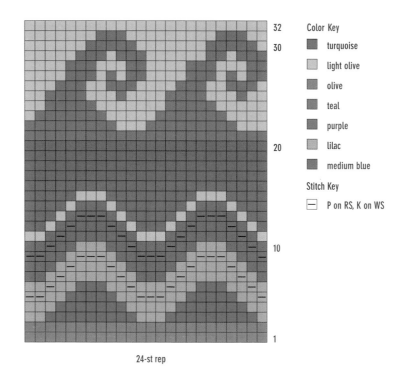

**Color Key**

- ■ turquoise
- ■ light olive
- ■ olive
- ■ teal
- ■ purple
- ■ lilac
- ■ medium blue

**Stitch Key**

☐ P on RS, K on WS

24-st rep

77

# fair isle/multicolor

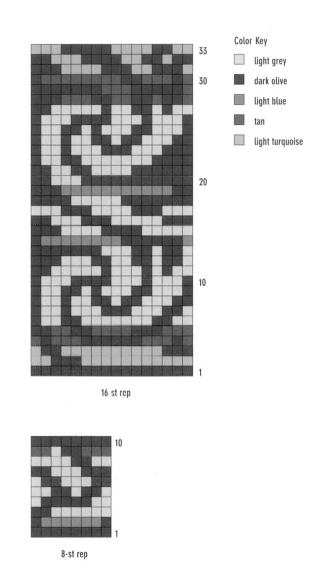

Color Key

- light grey
- dark olive
- light blue
- tan
- light turquoise

16 st rep

8-st rep

# fair isle/multicolor

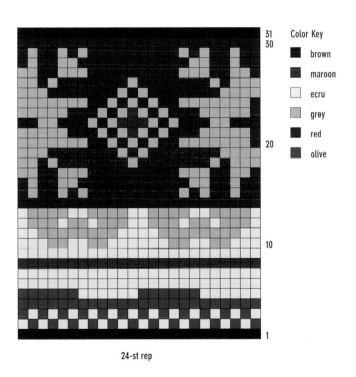

**Color Key**

- ■ brown
- ■ maroon
- □ ecru
- ■ grey
- ■ red
- ■ olive

24-st rep

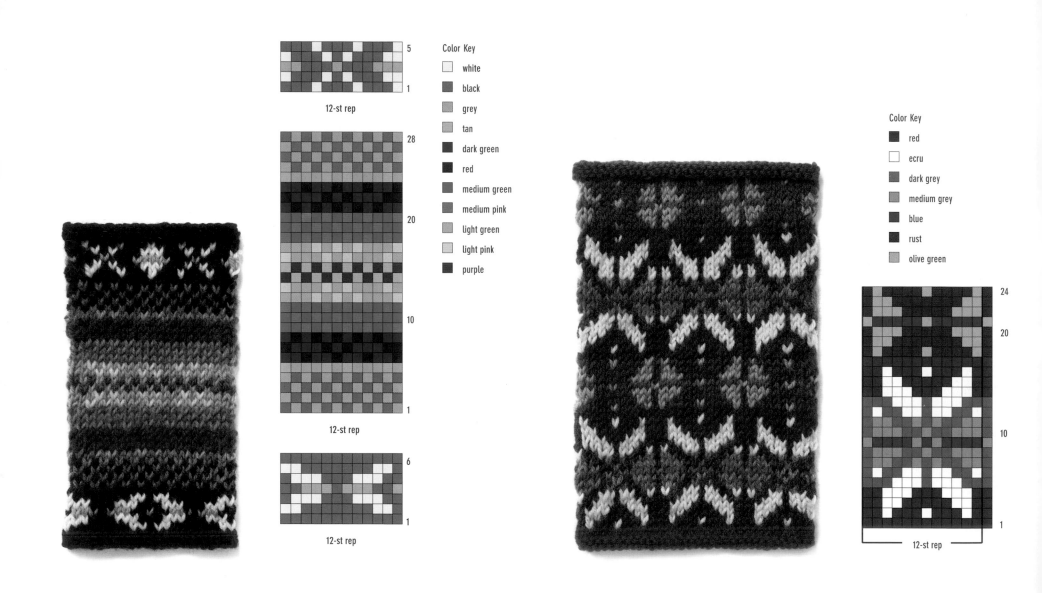

**Color Key**

- white
- black
- grey
- tan
- dark green
- red
- medium green
- medium pink
- light green
- light pink
- purple

12-st rep

**Color Key**

- red
- ecru
- dark grey
- medium grey
- blue
- rust
- olive green

12-st rep

# fair isle/multicolor

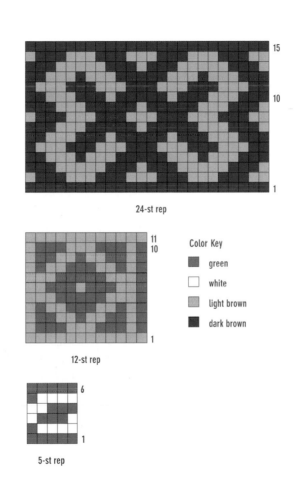

24-st rep

11
10

1

12-st rep

**Color Key**

■ green

□ white

■ light brown

■ dark brown

6

1

5-st rep

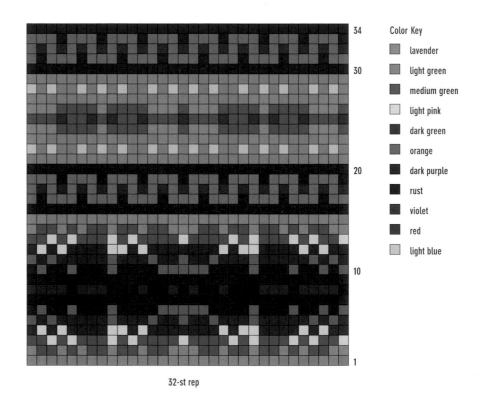

34

30

20

10

1

**Color Key**

lavender

light green

medium green

light pink

dark green

orange

dark purple

rust

violet

red

light blue

**32-st rep**

intarsia/motifs

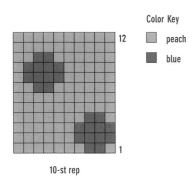

Color Key

- ☐ peach
- ■ blue

12

1

10-st rep

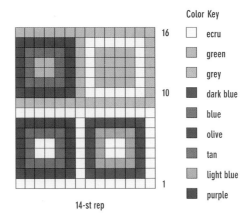

Color Key

- ☐ ecru
- ☐ green
- ☐ grey
- ■ dark blue
- ■ blue
- ■ olive
- ■ tan
- ☐ light blue
- ■ purple

16

10

1

14-st rep

85

86

# intarsia/motifs

**Color Key**

- ☐ white
- ■ blue
- ☐ yellow
- ■ red
- ■ green

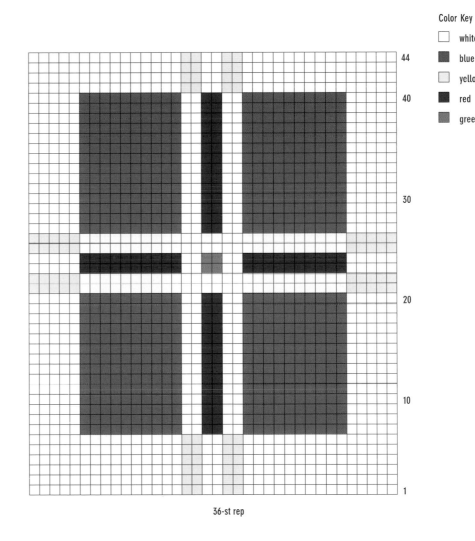

44
40
30
20
10
1

36-st rep

## Color Key

- ☐ ecru
- ■ lilac
- ■ green
- ■ mint
- ■ purple
- ☒ duplicate st in green
- ☒ duplicate st in mint
- ☒ duplicate st in purple

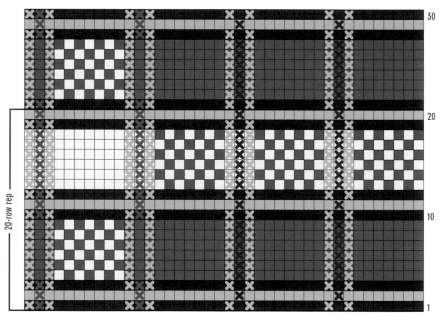

20-row rep

40-st rep

88

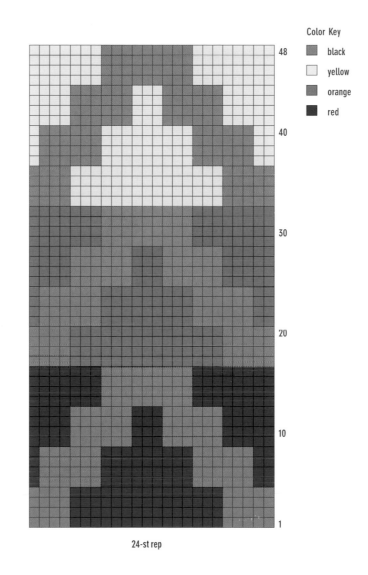

**Color Key**

- black
- yellow
- orange
- red

48

40

30

20

10

1

24-st rep

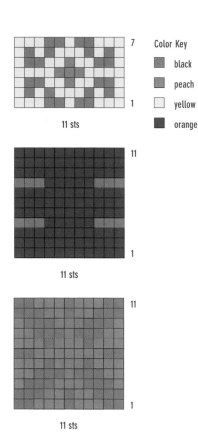

Color Key

black

peach

yellow

orange

11 sts

11 sts

11 sts

# intarsia/motifs

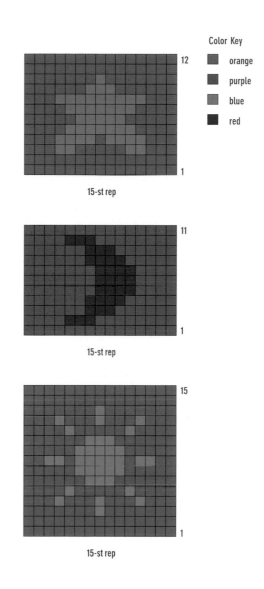

Color Key

- orange
- purple
- blue
- red

12

1

15-st rep

11

1

15-st rep

15

1

15-st rep

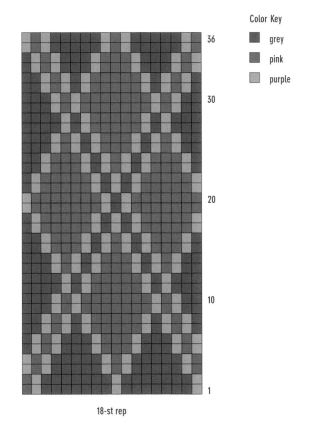

Color Key

- ■ grey
- ■ pink
- □ purple

36

30

20

10

1

18-st rep

# intarsia/motifs

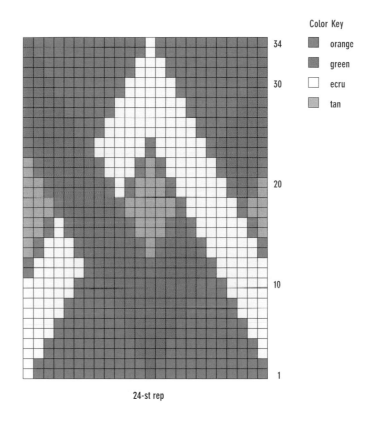

Color Key

- orange
- green
- ecru
- tan

34
30
20
10
1

24-st rep

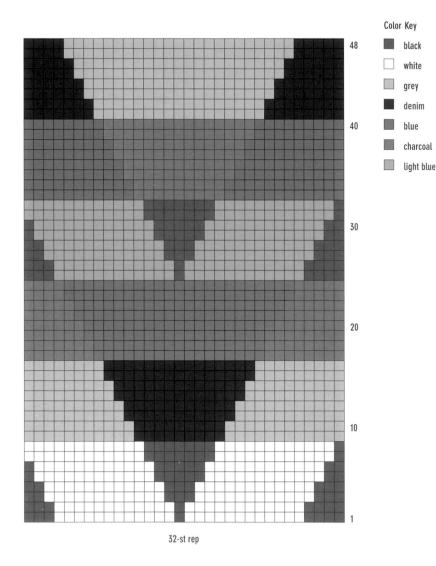

**Color Key**

- ■ black
- □ white
- ■ grey
- ■ denim
- ■ blue
- ■ charcoal
- ■ light blue

48

40

30

20

10

1

32-st rep

94

# intarsia/motifs

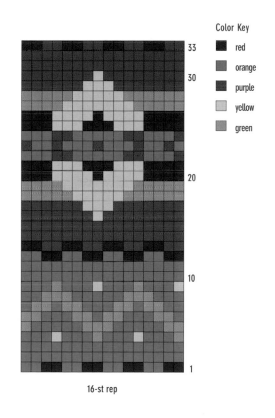

Color Key
- red
- orange
- purple
- yellow
- green

33
30

20

10

1

16-st rep

95

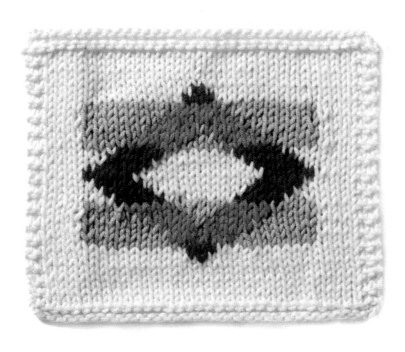

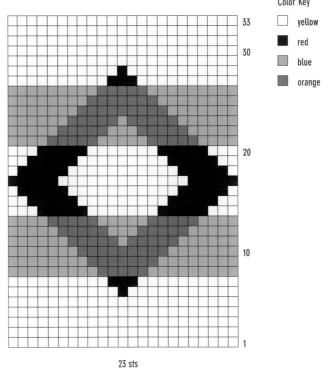

Color Key

☐ yellow

■ red

▨ blue

▨ orange

33
30

20

10

1

23 sts

# intarsia/motifs

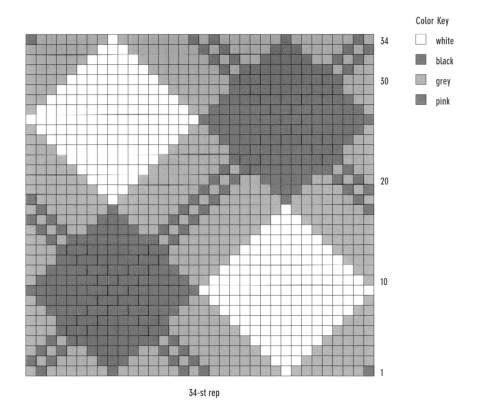

**Color Key**

- ☐ white
- ■ black
- ☐ grey
- ■ pink

34

30

20

10

1

**34-st rep**

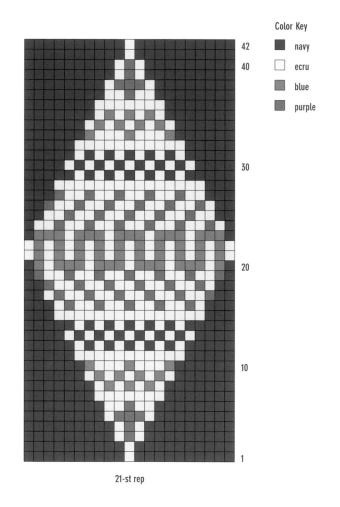

Color Key

- ■ navy
- □ ecru
- ■ blue
- ■ purple

42
40
30
20
10
1

**21-st rep**

# intarsia/motifs

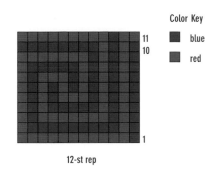

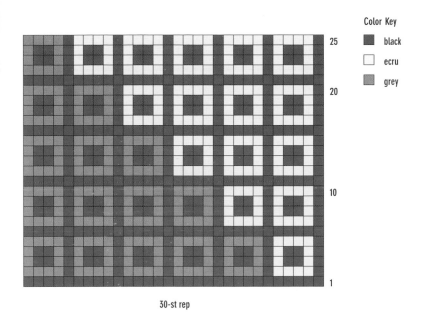

Color Key

■ black

□ ecru

■ grey

30-st rep

Color Key

■ blue

■ red

12-st rep

99

100

**Color Key**

- charcoal
- blue
- ecru
- black
- red
- grey

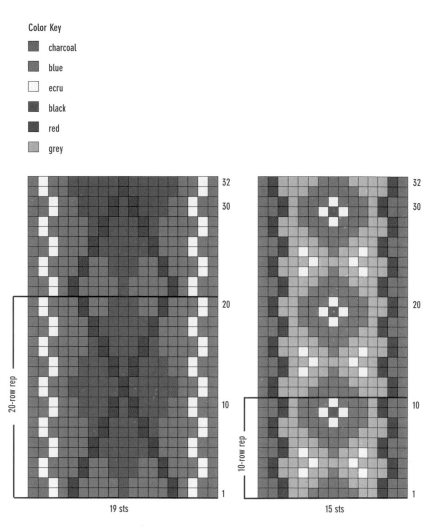

20-row rep

19 sts

10-row rep

15 sts

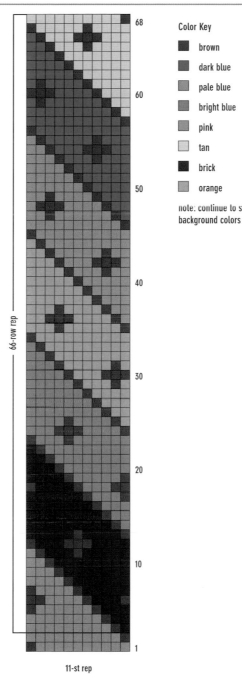

**Color Key**

- ■ brown
- ■ dark blue
- ■ pale blue
- ■ bright blue
- ■ pink
- □ tan
- ■ brick
- ■ orange

note: continue to shift brown accent and
background colors 1 st to the left and 1 row up

66-row rep

11-st rep

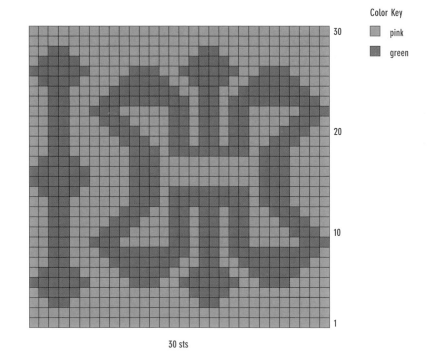

Color Key

pink

green

30

20

10

1

30 sts

## 104 making waves

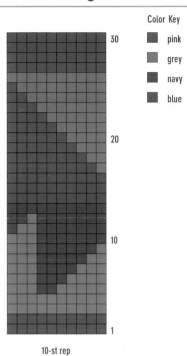

**Color Key**
- ■ pink
- ■ grey
- ■ navy
- ■ blue

30

20

10

1

10-st rep

## 105 english rose

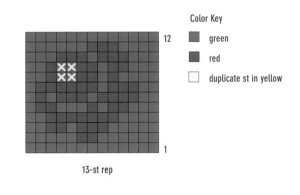

**Color Key**
- ■ green
- ■ red
- ☐ duplicate st in yellow

12

1

13-st rep

104

105

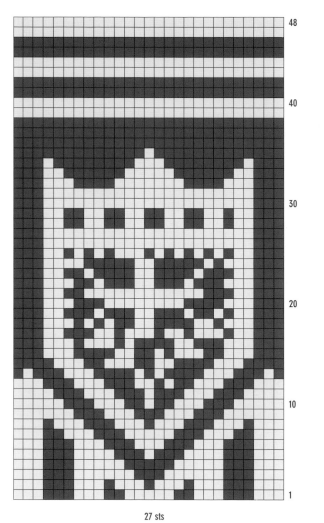

**Color Key**

■ blue

□ yellow

48

40

30

20

10

1

27 sts

# intarsia/motifs

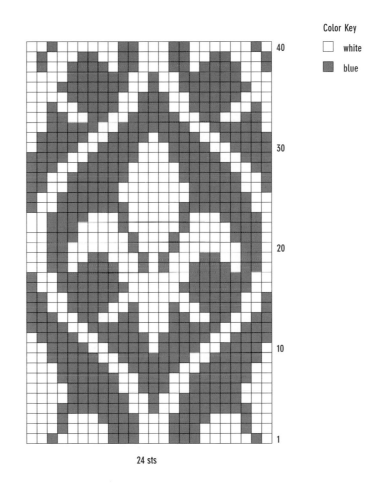

Color Key

☐ white

▨ blue

40

30

20

10

1

24 sts

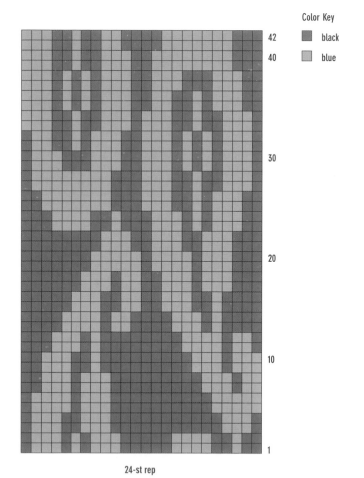

**Color Key**

◼ black

◼ blue

42
40

30

20

10

1

24-st rep

108

## 109 sparkle

## 110 flicker

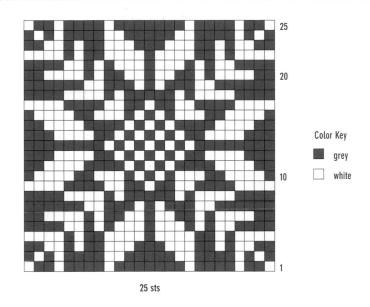

25 sts

### Color Key

■ grey

□ white

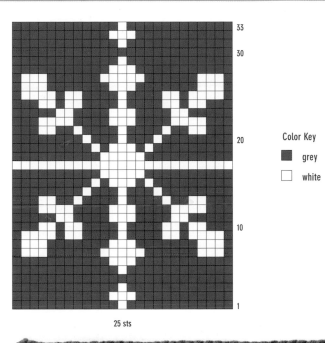

25 sts

### Color Key

■ grey

□ white

**109**

**110**

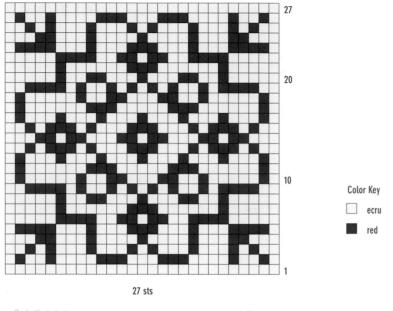

27

20

10

1

27 sts

Color Key

☐ ecru

■ red

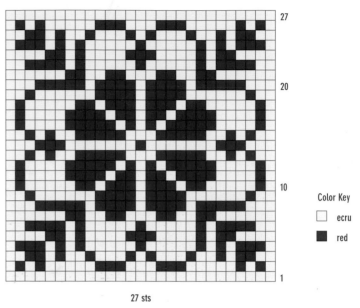

27

20

10

1

27 sts

Color Key

☐ ecru

■ red

111

112

## 113 pomegranate

## 114 nordic star

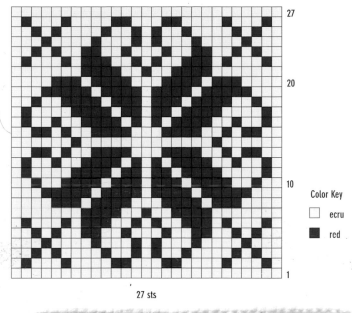

27

20

10

1

27 sts

**Color Key**

☐ ecru

■ red

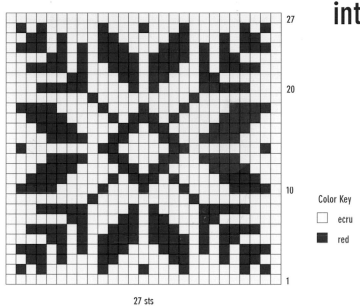

27

20

10

1

27 sts

**Color Key**

☐ ecru

■ red

113

114

## 115 floating buds

## 116 lattice bud

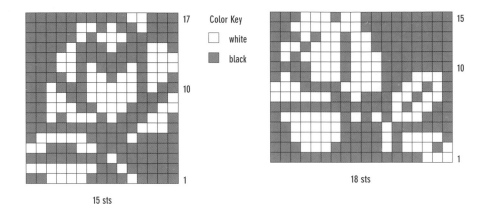

15 sts

18 sts

Color Key
- ☐ white
- ▨ black

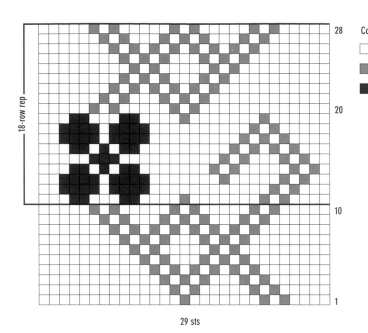

18-row rep.

29 sts

Color Key
- ☐ white
- ▨ black
- ■ red

115

116

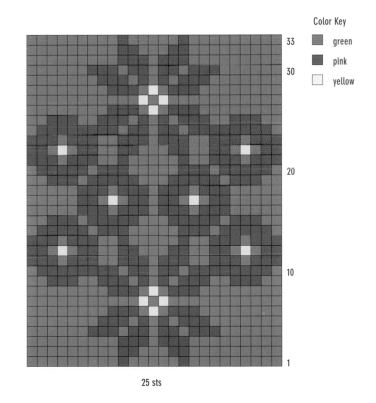

**Color Key**

green

pink

yellow

33

30

20

10

1

25 sts

117

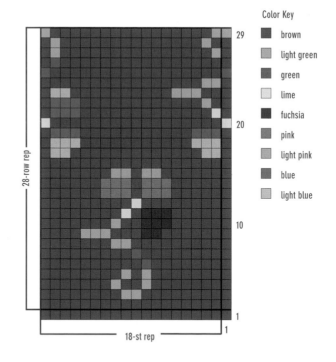

**Color Key**

- brown
- light green
- green
- lime
- fuchsia
- pink
- light pink
- blue
- light blue

28-row rep

18-st rep

118

# intarsia/motifs

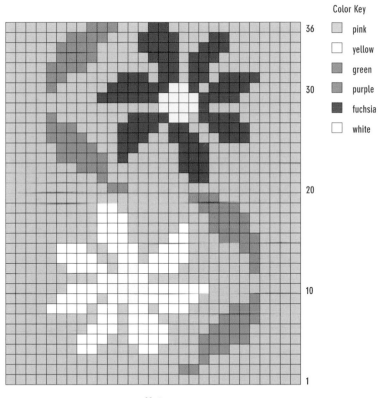

**Color Key**

- pink
- yellow
- green
- purple
- fuchsia
- white

36

30

20

10

1

29 sts

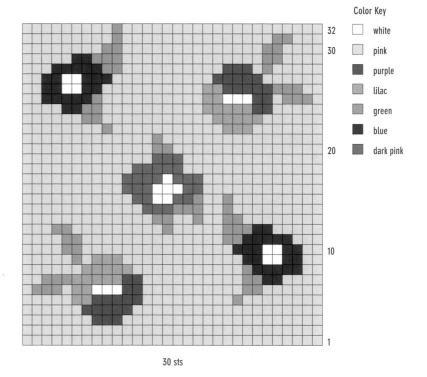

**Color Key**

- ☐ white
- ☐ pink
- ■ purple
- ■ lilac
- ■ green
- ■ blue
- ■ dark pink

32
30

20

10

1

30 sts

**120**

# intarsia/motifs

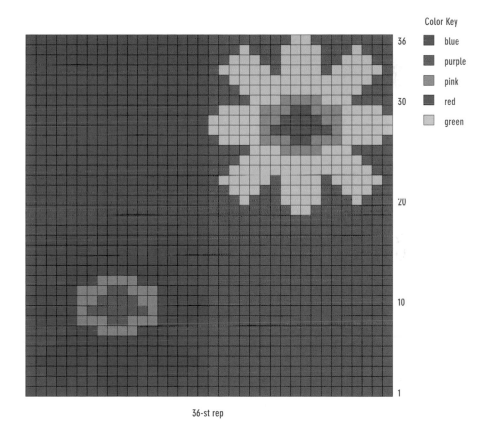

Color Key

■ blue
■ purple
■ pink
■ red
■ green

36

30

20

10

1

36-st rep

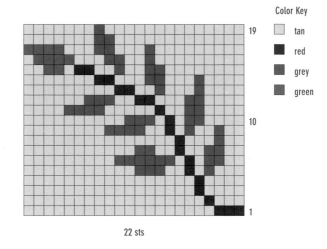

**Color Key**

- tan
- red
- grey
- green

22 sts

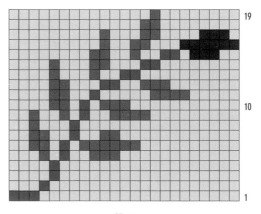

23 sts

122

# intarsia/motifs

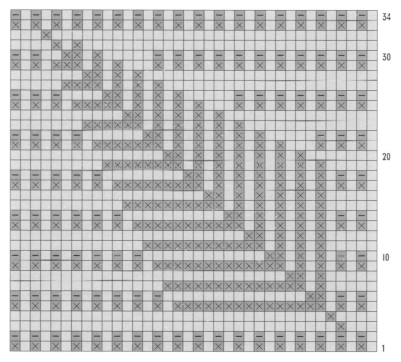

**Color Key**

- ☐ tan
- ▨ black

**Stitch Key**

- ☒ K on RS, P on WS with black
- ⊟ P on RS, K on WS with black

34

30

20

10

1

36 sts

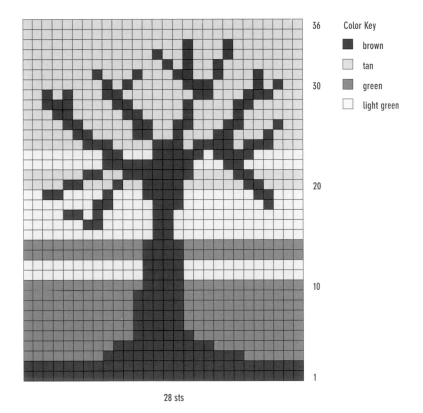

**Color Key**

- brown
- tan
- green
- light green

36

30

20

10

1

28 sts

# intarsia/motifs

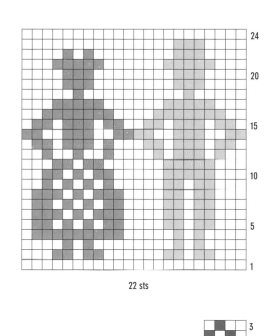

**Color Key**

- ☐ white
- ■ black
- ☐ light grey
- ■ dark grey

22 sts

3
1

4-st rep

125

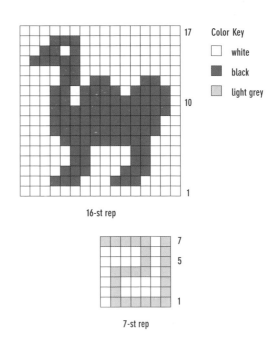

Color Key

☐ white

■ black

☐ light grey

16-st rep

7-st rep

# intarsia/motifs

**Color Key**

- ■ dark blue
- □ white
- ■ blue
- ⊡ make bobble: K into front, back, front, back and front of st, turn, p5, turn, k5, turn, p2tog, p1, p2tog, turn, k3tog

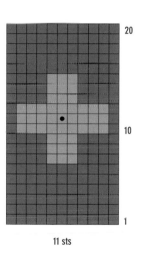 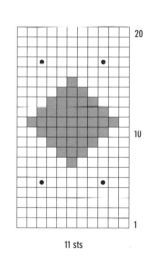 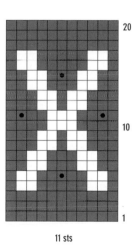

11 sts      11 sts      11 sts

127

Stitch Key

☐ K on RS, p on WS

⊟ P on RS, k on WS

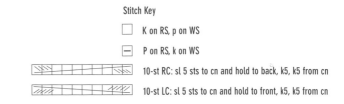 10-st RC: sl 5 sts to cn and hold to back, k5, k5 from cn

10-st LC: sl 5 sts to cn and hold to front, k5, k5 from cn

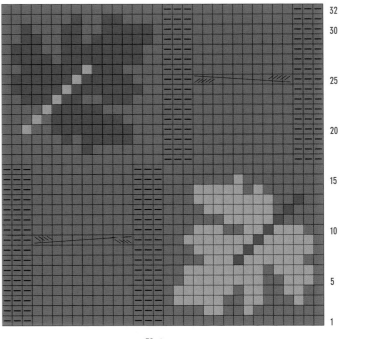

Color Key

■ raspberry

■ green

■ red

32-st rep

128

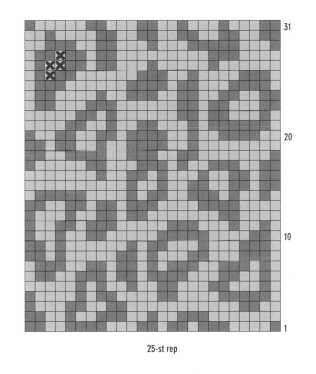

**Color Key**

- camel
- black
- ☒ duplicate stitch in red (as desired)

25-st rep

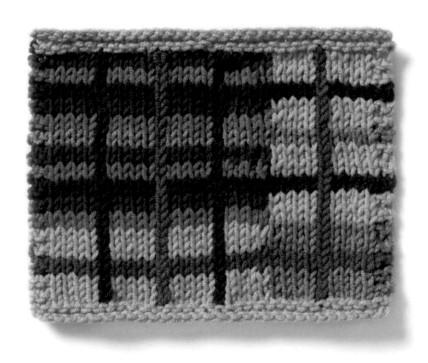

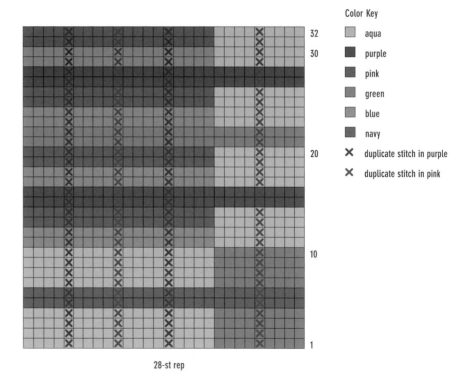

**Color Key**

- aqua
- purple
- pink
- green
- blue
- navy
- ✗ duplicate stitch in purple
- ✗ duplicate stitch in pink

32
30
20
10
1

28-st rep

130

adding texture

# 131 cornflower rows

(over any number of sts)

Row 1 (RS) With B, purl.

Row 2 With B, knit.

Rows 3 and 4 With A, purl.

Row 5 With A, knit.

Row 6 With A, purl.

Row 7 With B, purl.

Row 8 With B, knit.

Rows 9 and 10 With A, purl.

Row 11 With A, knit.

Row 12 With A, purl.

Row 13 With B, purl.

Row 14 With B, knit.

Rows 15 and 16 With C, purl.

Row 17 With C, knit.

Row 18 With C, purl.

Row 19 With B, purl.

Row 20 With B, knit.

Rows 21 and 22 With A, purl.

Row 23 With A, knit.

Row 24 With A, purl.

Row 25 With A, knit.

Row 26 With A, purl.

Rep rows 1–26.

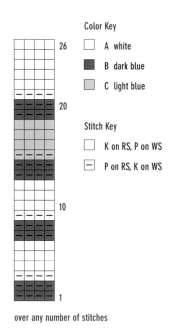

**Color Key**

☐ A  white

■ B  dark blue

▨ C  light blue

**Stitch Key**

☐ K on RS, P on WS

⊟ P on RS, K on WS

over any number of stitches

(multiple of 6 sts plus 1)

Rows 1, 3 and 5 With B, *k1, p5; rep from *, end k1.

Rows 2, 4 and 6 With B, p1, *k5, p1; rep from * to end.

Rows 7 and 9 With A, *k1, p5; rep from *, end k1.

Rows 8 and 10 With A, p1, *k5, p1; rep from * to end.

Row 11 With C, *k1, p5; rep from *, end k1.

Row 12 With C, p1, *k5, p1; rep from * to end.

Rows 13, 15 and 17 With A, *k1, p5; rep from *, end k1.

Rows 14, 16 and 18 With A, p1, *k5, p1; rep from * to end.

Rows 19 and 21 With C, *k1, p5; rep from *, end k1.

Rows 20 and 22 With C, p1, *k5, p1; rep from * to end.

Row 23 With B, *k1, p5; rep from *, end k1.

Row 24 With B, p1, *k5, p1; rep from * to end.

Rows 25, 27 and 29 With C, *k1, p5; rep from *, end k1.

Rows 26, 28 and 30 With C, p1, *k5, p1; rep from * to end.

Rows 31 and 33 With B, *k1, p5; rep from *, end k1.

Rows 32 and 34 With B, p1, *k5, p1; rep from * to end.

Row 35 With A, *k1, p5; rep from *, end k1.

Row 36 With A, p1, *k5, p1; rep from * to end.

Rep rows 1–36.

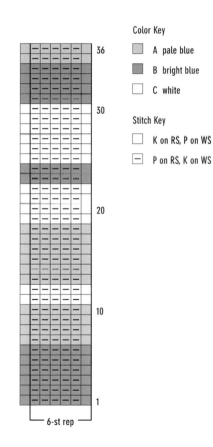

**Color Key**

A pale blue

B bright blue

C white

**Stitch Key**

K on RS, P on WS

— P on RS, K on WS

6-st rep

## 133 woven plaid

MC (pale blue)

A (dark blue)

B (periwinkle)

(multiple of 2 sts plus 2)

**Row 1 (RS)** Wyif sl 1, *k1, wyif sl 1; rep from *, end k1.

**Row 2** Wyib sl 1, *p1, wyib sl 1; rep from *, end p1.

Rep rows 1 and 2 in stripe pat:

6 rows MC, *[2 rows A, 2 rows MC] twice, 16 rows MC, (2 rows B, 2 rows MC) twice, 4 rows MC, [2 rows A, 2 rows MC] twice, 4 rows MC, (2 rows B, 2 rows MC) twice, 16 rows MC; rep from * to desired length.

### Vertical stripes

Vertical plaid stripes are worked by weaving contrasting yarn into the knitted piece.

To work vertical plaid stripes, weave yarn under the horizontal bar of each st on each row.

When weaving more than 1 vertical stripe, cut one continuous strand for desired number of stripes. Cut strand the length of the piece you are weaving, plus an extra 5".

After weaving, piece will become wider and shorter than original piece, knit and weave swatch to gauge final dimensions.

Work vertical stripe from right to left as follows; weave 4 sts with B, 1 st with A, leave 16 sts unwoven — 21-st rep.

133

(multiple of 24 sts)
Row 1 With A, knit.
Row 2 With MC, purl.
Row 3 With B, knit.
Row 4 With MC, purl.
Row 5 With C, knit.
Row 6 With MC, purl.
Row 7 With B, knit.
Row 8 With MC, purl.
Row 9 With A, knit.
Rows 10 to 24 Work in St st with MC.
Rep rows 1–24.

**Vertical Stripes**

With B, work duplicate st over st 10 in row 2, *skip next row, work duplicate st over st 10 of next row; rep from * to top edge. Rep with st 12. With A, work duplicate st over st 22 in row 2, *skip next row, work duplicate st over st 22 of next row; rep from * to top edge. Rep with st 24.

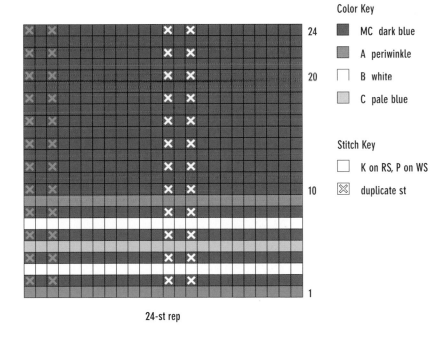

**Color Key**

◼ MC  dark blue

◼ A  periwinkle

☐ B  white

◼ C  pale blue

**Stitch Key**

☐ K on RS, P on WS

⊠ duplicate st

24-st rep

(over any number of sts)

Row 1 (RS) With E, knit.

Row 2 With E, knit.

Rows 3–6 With C, knit.

Rows 7–14 With A, knit.

Rows 15–20 With B, knit.

Row 21–24 With D, knit.

Rep rows 1–24.

**Weaving**

(instructions appear only in text, not on chart.)

When weaving more than 1 vertical stripe, cut a continuous strand for desired number of stripes. Cut strand to the length of the piece you are weaving, plus an extra 5".

Each garter st forms 2 lps, one going "up" and the other going "down", weave the up lps from bottom to top and down lps from top to bottom, to ensure even lines.

After weaving, piece will become wider and shorter than original piece, knit and weave swatch to gauge final dimensions.

**Vertical stripes**

Weave vertical stripe from right to left as foll: *2 lp D, 1 lps E, 2 lps C, 8 lps B, 8 lps A, 2 lps D; rep from * across—25 lps rep.

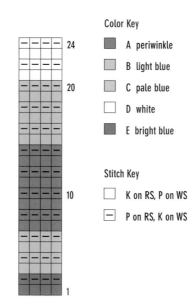

**Color Key**

A  periwinkle

B  light blue

C  pale blue

D  white

E  bright blue

**Stitch Key**

K on RS, P on WS

P on RS, K on WS

135

(multiple of 8 sts plus 4)

Rows 1, 3, 5 and 7 With A, knit.

Rows 2, 4, 6 and 8 With A, p2, *k4, p4; rep from *, end k2.

Rows 9, 11, 13 and 15 With B, knit.

Rows 10, 12, 14 and 16 With B, k2, *p4, k4; rep from *, end p2.

Rows 17, 19, 21, 23 With C, knit.

Rows 18, 20, 22, 24 With C, p2, *k4, p4; rep from *, end k2.

Rows 25, 27, 29, 31 With A, knit.

Rows 26, 28, 30, 32 With A, k2, *p4, k4; rep from *, end p2.

Rows 33, 35, 37, 39 With B, knit.

Rows 34, 36, 38, 40 With B, p2, *k4, p4; rep from *, end k2.

Rows 41, 43, 45, 47 With C, knit.

Rows 42, 44, 46, 48 With C, k2, *p4, k4; rep from *, end p2

Rep rows 1–48.

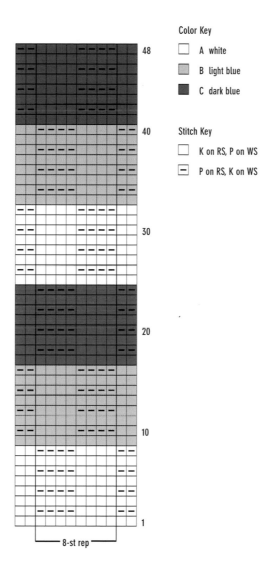

**Color Key**

☐ A white

☐ B light blue

☐ C dark blue

**Stitch Key**

☐ K on RS, P on WS

⊟ P on RS, K on WS

8-st rep

# 137 andes

MB (make bobble)

With B [k1, p1, k1] in next st, turn, p3, turn, k3, turn, p3, turn, k3tog.

(multiple of 22 sts)

Row 1 and 3 With A, knit.

Row 2 With A, purl.

Rows 4 and 5 With B, purl.

Row 6 With B, knit.

Rows 7–18 Rep rows 1–6 twice.

Row 19 *P13 B, k4 A, p1 B, k4 A; rep from * to end.

Row 20 P3 A, *k3 B, p4 A, k11 B, p4 A; rep from *, end p1 A.

Row 21 K2 A, *p9 B, k4 A, p5 B, k4 A; rep from *, end k2 A.

Row 22 P1 A, *k3 B, p1 A, k3 B, p4 A, k7 B, p4 A; rep from *, end p3 A.

Row 23 *K4 A, p5 B, k4 A, p3 B, k3 A, p3 B; rep from * to end.

Row 24 K2 B, *p5 A, k3 B, p4 A, k3 B, p4 A, k3 B; rep from *, end k1 B.

Row 25 P2 B, *k4 A, p1 B, k4 A, p3 B, k3 A, MB, k3 A, p3 B; rep from *, end p1 B.

Row 26 *P9 A, k3 B, p7 A, k3 B; rep from * to end.

Row 27 K1 A, *p3 B, k5 A, p3 B, [k3 A, MB] twice, k3 A; rep from *, end k2 A.

Row 28 P11 A, *k3 B, p3 A, k3 B, k13 A; rep from *, end k2 A.

Row 29 K3 A, *p3 B, k1 A, p3 B, k15 A; rep from *, end k12 A.

Row 30 P13 A, *k5 B, p17 A; rep from *, end p4 A.

Rows 31–42 Rep rows 1–6 twice.

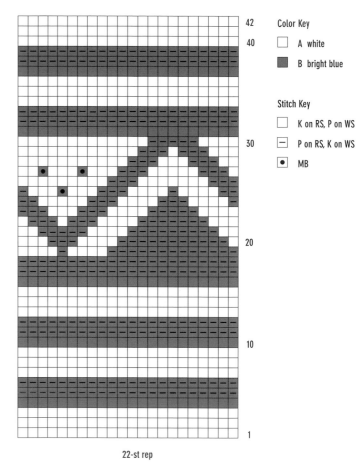

Color Key

☐ A white

■ B bright blue

Stitch Key

☐ K on RS, P on WS

⊟ P on RS, K on WS

⊡ MB

22-st rep

# 138 multi chevron

(multiple of 15 sts)

Rows 1 and 3 With A, *k2tog, k4, k into the front and back of next st, k1, k into the front and back of next st, k4, ssk; rep from * to end.

Rows 2 and 4 With A, knit.

Rows 5 and 7 With B, *k2tog, k4, k into the front and back of next st, k1, k into

the front and back of next st, k4, ssk; rep from * to end.

Rows 6 and 8 With B, knit.

Rows 9 and 11 With C, *k2tog, k4, k into the front and back of next st, k1, k into the front and back of next st, k4, ssk; rep from * to end.

Rows 10 and 12 With C, knit.

Rows 13 and 15 With D, *k2tog, k4, k into the front and back of next st, k1, k into the front and back of next st, k4, ssk; rep from * to end.

Rows 14 and 16 With D, knit.

Rows 17 and 19 With E, *k2tog, k4, k into the front and back of next st, k1, k into the front and back of next st, k4,

ssk; rep from * to end.

Rows 18 and 20 With E, knit.

Rows 21 and 23 With F, *k2tog, k4, k into the front and back of next st, k1, k into the front and back of next st, k4, ssk; rep from * to end.

Rows 22 and 24 With F, knit.

Repeat rows 1–24.

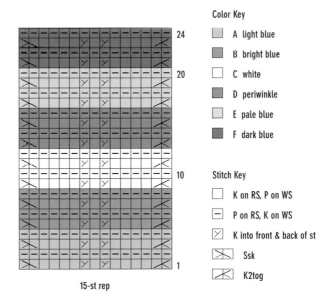

**Color Key**

| | |
|---|---|
| | A light blue |
| | B bright blue |
| | C white |
| | D periwinkle |
| | E pale blue |
| | F dark blue |

**Stitch Key**

| | |
|---|---|
| | K on RS, P on WS |
| — | P on RS, K on WS |
| ⊠ | K into front & back of st |
| ⊠ | Ssk |
| ⊠ | K2tog |

15-st rep

138

## 139 subtle spots

(multiple of 6 sts plus 3)
Row 1 *K3 A, k3 B; rep from *, end k3 A.
Row 2 P3 A, *p3 B, p3 A; rep from * to end.
Row 3 With A, *k3, p3; rep from *, end k3.
Row 4 With A, p3, *k3, p3; rep from * to end.
Row 5 With A, knit.
Row 6 With A, purl.
Repeat rows 1–6.

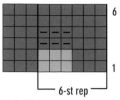

6-st rep

### Color Key

■ A  dark blue

■ B  pale blue

### Stitch Key

☐  K on RS, P on WS

─  P on RS, K on WS

**139**

## 140 rope swing

8-st LC Sl 4 sts to cn and hold to front
of work, k4, k4 from cn.
(multiple of 16 sts plus 8)
Rows 1, 3, 7 and 9 (RS) *K8 A, k8 B;
rep from *, end k8 A.
Row 2 and all WS rows P8 A, *p8 B,
p8 A; rep from * to end.
Row 5 *8-st LC with A, k8 B, rep from
*, end 8-st LC with A.
Row 11 *K8 A, 8-st LC with B, rep
from *, end k8 A.
Row 12 Rep row 2.
Rep rows 1–12.

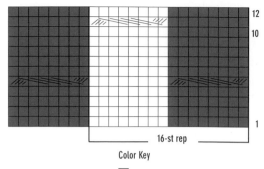

16-st rep

### Color Key

■ A  bright blue

☐  B  white

### Stitch Key

☐  K on RS, P on WS

▨▨▨▨  8-st LC

**140**

(multiple of 15 sts)

Row 1 (RS) With MC, knit.

Row 2 With MC, purl.

Row 3 *K3 MC, p3 A, k3 MC, p6 A; rep from * to end.

Row 4 *P6 B, p3 MC, p3 B, p3 MC; rep from * to end.

Row 5 *K3 MC, p3 B, k3 MC, p6 B; rep from * to end.

Row 6 *P6 A, p3 MC, p3 A, p3 MC; rep from * to end.

Row 7 With MC *k3, p3, k3, p6; rep from * to end.

Rows 8 and 10 With MC, purl.

Row 9 With MC, knit.

Row 11 *K3 MC, p6 C, k3 MC, p3 C; rep from * to end.

Row 12 *P3 D, p3 MC, p6 D, p3 MC; rep from * to end.

Row 13 *K3 MC, p6 D, k3 MC, p3 D; rep from * to end.

Row 14 *P3 C, p3 MC, p6 C, p3 MC; rep from * to end.

Row 15 With MC *k3, p6, k3, p3; rep from * to end.

Rows 16 and 18 With MC, purl.

Row 17 With MC, knit.

Row 19 *K3 MC, p3 B, k3 MC, p6 B; rep from * to end.

Row 20 *P6 A, p3 MC, p3 A, p3 MC; rep from * to end.

Row 21 *K3 MC, p3 A, k3 MC, p6 A; rep from * to end.

Row 22 *P6 B, p3 MC, p3 B, p3 MC; rep from * to end.

Row 23 With MC *k3, p3, k3, p6; rep from * to end.

Rows 24 and 26 With MC, purl.

Row 25 With MC, knit.

Row 27 *K3 MC, p6 D, k3 MC, p3 D; rep from * to end.

Row 28 *P3 C, p3 MC, p6 C, p3 MC; rep from * to end.

Row 29 *K3 MC, p6 C, k3 MC, p3 C; rep from * to end.

Row 30 *P3 D, p3 MC, p6 D, p3 MC; rep from * to end.

Row 31 With MC *k3, p6, k3, p3; rep from * to end.

Row 32 With MC, purl.

Rep rows 1–32.

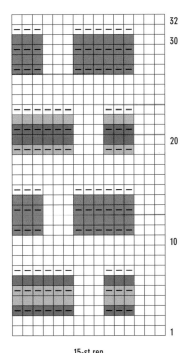

**15-st rep**

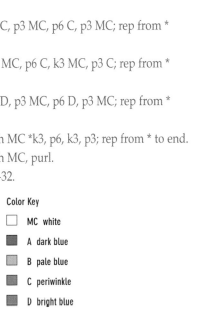

**Color Key**

| | |
|---|---|
| ☐ | MC white |
| ■ | A dark blue |
| ■ | B pale blue |
| ■ | C periwinkle |
| ■ | D bright blue |

**Stitch Key**

| | |
|---|---|
| ☐ | K on RS, P on WS |
| − | P on RS, K on WS |

141

(multiple of 8 sts plus 9)

Row 1 (RS) With MC, knit.

Row 2 With MC, purl.

Row 3 With A k2, wyib sl 1, *k1, [k1, yo, k1, yo, k1 into next st], k1, wyib sl 5; rep from *, end k1, [k1,yo, k1, yo, k1 into next st], k1, wyib sl 1, k2.

Row 4 With A, p2, wyif sl 1, p1, [p1, wrapping yarn twice around needle] 5 times, p1, *wyif sl 5, p1, [p1, wrapping yarn twice around needle] 5 times, p1; rep from *, end wyif sl 1, p2.

Row 5 With MC, k3, *k1, [wyib sl 5, dropping extra wraps], k6; rep from *, end k1, [wyib sl 5, dropping extra wraps], k4.

Row 6 With MC, p4, wyif sl 5, p1, *p6, wyif sl 5, p1; rep from *, end p3.

Row 7 With MC, k3, *k2tog, wyib sl 3, ssk, k5; rep from *, end k2tog, wyib sl 3, ssk, k3.

Row 8 With MC, p4, wyif sl 3, p1, *p6, wyif sl 3, p1; rep from *, end p3.

Row 9 With MC, k3, *k2tog, wyib sl 1, ssk, k5; rep from *, end k2tog, wyib sl 1, ssk, k3.

Row 10 With MC, p4, wyif sl 1, p1, *p6, wyif sl 1, p1; rep from *, end p3.

Rows 11–18 With MC, work in St st.

Row 19 With B, k2, *wyib sl 5, k1, [k1, yo, k1, yo, k1 into next st], k1; rep from *, end wyib sl 5, k2.

Row 20 With B, p2, wyif sl 5, *p1, [p1, wrapping yarn twice around needle] 5 times, p1, wyif sl 5; rep from *, end p2.

Row 21 With MC, k2, *k6, [wyib sl 5, dropping extra wraps], k1; rep from *, end k7.

Row 22 With MC, p7, *p1, wyif sl 5, p6, rep from *, end p2.

Row 23 With MC, k2, *k5, k2tog, wyib sl 3, ssk; rep from *, end k7.

Row 24 With MC, p7, *p1, wyif sl 3, p6; rep from *, end p2.

Row 25 With MC, k2, *k5, k2tog, wyib sl 1, ssk; rep from *, end k7.

Row 26 With MC, p7, *p1, wyif sl 1, p6; rep from *, end p2.

Rows 27–32 With MC, work in St st. Rep rows 1–32, working [rows 3 and 4 in C, rows 19 and 20 in A] once, then [rows 3 and 4 in B, rows 19 and 20 in C] once.

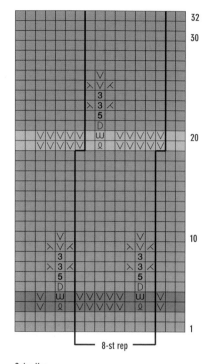

8-st rep

**Color Key**

▨ MC  periwinkle

▨ A  medium blue

▨ B  light blue

☐ C  white

**Stitch Key**

▽ wyib sl 1 on RS, wyif sl 1 on RS

╱ k2tog

╲ ssk

ɯ [p1, wrapping yarn twice around needle] 5 times

Ω k1, yo, k1, yo, k1 into next st

D wyib sl 5 sts, drop extra wraps

5 wyif sl 5

3 wyib sl 3 on RS, wyif sl 3 on WS

## 143 stripey

(any number of sts)

Row 1 (RS) With B, knit.

Rows 2 and 4 With B, knit.

Row 3 With B, purl.

Rows 5, 7 and 9 With A, knit.

Rows 6, 8 and 10 With A, purl.

Rep rows 1–10.

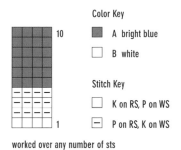

**Color Key**

■ A bright blue

□ B white

**Stitch Key**

□ K on RS, P on WS

— P on RS, K on WS

worked over any number of sts

## 144 pucker up

A (lt blue)

B (dark blue)

C (bright blue)

**M2P (make 2 puckers)** Hold RH needle to back of work, [pick up next st of previous color from 6 rows below and k this st tog with next st of current color on LH needle] twice.

(multiple of 36 sts)

With A cast on and work in St st for 6 rows. Change to B and work in St st for 6 rows.

Row 1 (RS) *With A, *M2P, k5, M2P, k3; rep from * to end.

Rows 6–10 With A, work in St st.

Row 7 With C, *k8, M2P, k6, M2P; rep from * to end.

Rows 8–12 With C, work in St st.

Row 13 With A, *k2, M2P, k8, M2P, k4; rep from * to end.

Rows 14–18 With A, work in St st.

Row 19 With B, *k5, M2P, k3, M2P; rep from * to end.

Rows 20–23 With B, work in St st.

Row 24 With B, purl.

Rep rows 1–24.

143

144

## 145 shadow boxing

(over an even number of sts)

Row 1 (RS) With A, purl.

Row 2 With A, knit.

Row 3 With B, k1, *k1, wyib sl 1; rep from *, end k1.

Row 4 With B, k1, *wyif sl 1, k1; rep from *, end k1.

Row 5 With A, k1, *yo, k2tog; rep from *, end k1.

Row 6 With A, purl.

Rep rows 1–6.

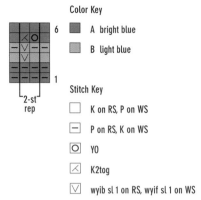

Color Key

■ A bright blue

■ B light blue

Stitch Key

☐ K on RS, P on WS

— P on RS, K on WS

⊙ YO

⊠ K2tog

☑ wyib sl 1 on RS, wyif sl 1 on WS

## 146 scalloped shell

(multiple of 10 sts plus 1)

Row 1 (RS) With A, knit.

Row 2 With A, purl.

Rows 3 and 4 With B, knit.

Row 5 With B, *k1, [yo, k1] twice, [k1 wrapping yarn twice around needle] 5 times, [k1, yo] twice; rep from *, end k1.

Row 6 With B, k1, *k4, wyif sl 5 dropping extra wraps, k5; rep from * to end.

Row 7 With A, *k5, wyib sl 5, k4; rep from *, end k1.

Row 8 With A, p1, *p4, p5tog, p5; rep from * to end.

Rep rows 1–8.

Color Key

■ A periwrinkle

☐ B white

Stitch Key

☐ K on RS, P on WS

— P on RS, K on WS

⊙ YO

00 K 1 wrapping yarn twice around needle

☑ wyib sl 1 on RS, wyif sl 1 on WS

▨ no stitch

P5tog

## 147 peruvian lace

(multiple of 4 sts plus 2)
**Cross 4** Wyib sl 4 dropping extra yo's, slip these 4 sts back to LH needle, then [k1, p1, k1, p1] into all 4 sts held tog.
**Row 1 (RS)** With A, knit.
**Row 2** With A, knit.
**Row 3** With B, k1, *k1 wrapping yarn twice around needle; rep from *, end k1.
**Row 4** With B, k1, *Cross 4; rep from *, end k1.
**Rows 5–8** With A, knit.
**Row 9** With A, k1, *k1 wrapping yarn twice around needle; rep from *, end k1.
**Row 10** With A, knit dropping extra wraps.
Rep rows 1–10.

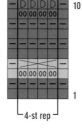

**Color Key**
■ A dark blue
□ B pale blue

**Stitch Key**
□ K on RS, P on WS
— P on RS, K on WS
|00| K 1 wrapping yarn twice
|D| K 1 dropping extra yo's
⊠ Cross 4

## 148 piped stripes

# adding texture

A (white)
B (periwinkle)
C (pale blue)
(multiple of 8 sts plus 2)
**Row 1 (RS)** With A, knit.
**Row 2** Sl first st to holder, *p2 B, p2 A; rep from * to last st, sl last st to holder.
**Rows 3 and 5** *K2 A, k2 B; rep from * to end.
**Rows 4 and 6** *P2 B, p2 A; rep from * to end.
**Piping row 7 (RS)** With a spare needle, pick up purl bumps along WS of row 1 (A row), making sure to pick up same number of sts as are on needle. Hold working needle to WS. With A, k st from holder, then *k tog 1 st from working needle with 1 st from spare needle; rep from * to end, k last st from holder.
**Rows 8 and 10** P3 C, *k4 A, p4 C; rep from *, end p3 C.
**Rows 9 and 11** K3 C, * p4 A, k4 C; rep from *, end k3 C.
**Row 12** Rep row 8.
Rep rows 1–12.

# 149 daisy chain

(multiple of 6 sts plus 1)

*Cluster st Wyif sl 5, dropping extra 2 wraps, [bring yarn to back between needles, sl 5 sts back to LH needle, bring yarn to front between needles, sl 5 sts to RH needle] twice.

Row 1 (RS) With A, knit.

Row 2 With A, knit.

Row 3 With A, k1, *[k1 wrapping yarn 3 times around needle] 5 times, k1; rep from * to end.

Row 4 With A *k1, Cluster st; rep from *, end k1.

Rows 5 and 6 With A, knit.

Rows 7 and 9 With B, knit.

Rows 8 and 10 With B, purl.

Rows 11 and 12 With A, knit.

Row 13 With A, k4, *[k1, wrapping yarn 3 times around needle] 5 times, k1; rep from *, end k3.

Row 14 With A, k3, *k1, Cluster st; rep from *, end k4.

Rows 15 and 16 With A, knit.

Rows 17 and 19 With B, knit.

Rows 18 and 20 With B, purl.

Rep rows 1–20.

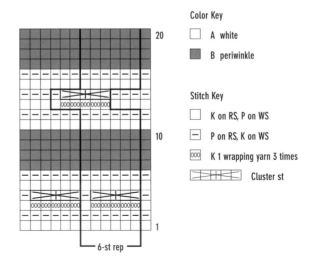

**Color Key**

☐ A white

▨ B periwinkle

**Stitch Key**

☐ K on RS, P on WS

⊟ P on RS, K on WS

⊠ K 1 wrapping yarn 3 times

⊞ Cluster st

6-st rep

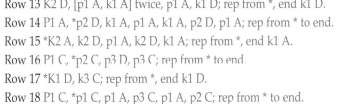

MB (make bobble) With A, [k1, p1, k1, p1] in 1 st, turn, p4tog, turn, wyif sl resulting st back to RH needle.

(multiple of 8 sts plus 1)

Rows 1 and 3 (RS) With B, *p1, k3; rep from *, end p1.

Row 2 P1 B, *p1 B, MB with A, p3 B, MB with A, p2 B; rep from * to end.

Row 4 P1 A, *k1 B, p1 B, k1 B, p1 A; rep from * to end.

Row 5 *K2 A, p1 B, k1 A; rep from *, end k1 A.

Row 6 P1 C, *p3 A, p1 C; rep from * to end.

Row 7 *K2 C, k1 A, k1 C; rep from *, end k1 C.

Row 8 P1 D, *p3 C, p1 D;  rep from * to end.

Row 9 *K3 C, k3 D, k2 C; rep from *, end k1 C.

Row 10 P1 A, *[p1 A, p2 D] twice, p2 A; rep from * to end.

Row 11 *K1 A, k2 D, k1 A, p1 A, k1 A, k2 D; rep from *, end k1 A.

Row 12 P1 D, *p1 D, [p1 A, k1 A] twice, p1 A, p2 D; rep from * to end.

Row 13 K2 D, [p1 A, k1 A] twice, p1 A, k1 D; rep from *, end k1 D.

Row 14 P1 A, *p2 D, k1 A, p1 A, k1 A, p2 D, p1 A; rep from * to end.

Row 15 *K2 A, k2 D, p1 A, k2 D, k1 A; rep from *, end k1 A.

Row 16 P1 C, *p2 C, p3 D, p3 C; rep from * to end.

Row 17 *K1 D, k3 C; rep from *, end k1 D.

Row 18 P1 C, *p1 C, p1 A, p3 C, p1 A, p2 C; rep from * to end.

Row 19 *K1 C, k3 A; rep from *, end k1 C.

Row 20 P1 A, *p1 A, p1 B, p3 A, p1 B, p2 A; rep from * to end.

Row 21 *K1 A, k1 B, p1 B, k1 B; rep from *, end k1 A.

Row 22 With B, p1, *k1, p1; rep from * to end.

Rows 23–25 Rep rows 1–3 once.

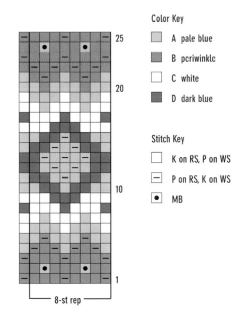

**Color Key**

- A  pale blue
- B  periwinkle
- C  white
- D  dark blue

**Stitch Key**

- K on RS, P on WS
- — P on RS, K on WS
- • MB

8-st rep

# 151 triumvirate

**Note** When crossing multicolored cables, keep colors in sequence as established. Use separate bobbins for each color in cable panel.

**MB (make bobble)** [K1, p1, k1, p1, k1, p1, k1] in next st, pass 6th st over 7th st, then pass 5th, 4th, 3rd, 2nd and first sts, one at a time, over 7th st.

**3-st RPC** Sl next st to cn and hold to back of work, k2, p1 from cn.

**3-st LPC** Sl 2 sts to cn and hold to front of work, p1, k2 from cn.

**4-st RC** Sl 2 sts to cn and hold to back of work, k2, k2 from cn.

**5-st RPC** Sl 3 sts to cn and hold to back of work, k2, sl p st from cn to LH needle and p1, k2 from cn.

**5-st LPC** Sl 3 sts to cn and hold to front of work, k2, sl p st from cn to LH needle and p1, k2 from cn.

**outer panel** (worked over 13 sts with B)
**Preparation row (WS)** K4, p2, k1, p2, k4.
**Row 1 (RS)** P4, 5-st RPC, p4.
**Row 2** K4, p2, k1, p2, k4.
**Row 3** P3, 3-st RPC, p1, 3-st LPC, p3.
**Rows 4 and 10** [K3, p2] twice, k3.
**Row 5** P2, 3-st RPC, p3, 3-st LPC, p2.
**Rows 6 and 8** K2, p2, k5, p2, k2.
**Row 7** P2, k2, p5, k2, p2.
**Row 9** P2, 3-st LPC, p3, 3-st RPC, p2.
**Row 11** P3, 3-st LPC, p1, 3-st RPC, p3.
**Rows 12, 14, 16 and 18** K4, p2, k1, p2, k4.
**Rows 13 and 17** P4, 5-st RPC, p4.
**Row 15** P4, k2, p1, k2, p4.
**Row 19** P3, 3-st RPC, p1, 3-st LPC, p3.
**Rows 20 and 26** [K3, p2] twice, k3.
**Row 21** P2, 3-st RPC, p3, 3-st LPC, p2.
**Rows 22 and 24** K2, p2, k5, p2, k2.
**Row 23** P2, k2, p2, MB, p2, k2, p2.
**Row 25** P2, 3-st LPC, p3, 3-st RPC, p2.
**Row 27** P3, 3-st LPC, p1, 3-st RPC, p3.
**Rows 28** K4, p2, k1, p2, k4.
**Row 29** P4, 5-st RPC, p4.
**Row 30** K4, p2, k1, p2, k4.

**Row 31** P4, k2, p1, k2, p4.
**Row 32** K4, p2, k1, p2, k4.
Rep rows 1–32.

**center panel** (worked over 21 sts with A)
**Preparation row (WS)** P1 tbl, k3, p2, k2, p2, k1, p2, k2, p2, k3, p1 tbl.
**Row 1 (RS)** K1 tbl, p3, k2, p2, 5-st RPC, p2, k2, p3, k1 tbl.
**Row 2** P1 tbl, k3, p2, k2, p2, k1, p2, k2, p2, k3, p1 tbl.
**Row 3 and 11** K1 tbl, p3, [3-st LPC, 3-st RPC, p1] twice, p2, k1 tbl.
**Rows 4, 6, 12 and 14** P1 tbl, k4, p4, k3, p4, k4, p1 tbl.
**Row 5 and 13** K1 tbl, p4, 4-st RC, p3, 4-st RC, p4, k1 tbl.
**Row 7 and 15** K1 tbl, p3, [3-st RC, 3-st LC, p1] twice, p2, k1 tbl.
**Rows 8 and 10** P1 tbl, k3, [p2, k2, p2, k1] twice, k2, p1 tbl.
**Row 9** K1 tbl, p3, k2, p2, 5-st LPC, p2, k2, p3, k1 tbl.
**Row 16** P1 tbl, k3, p2, k2, p2, k1, p2, k2, p2, k3, p1 tbl.
Rep rows 1–16.

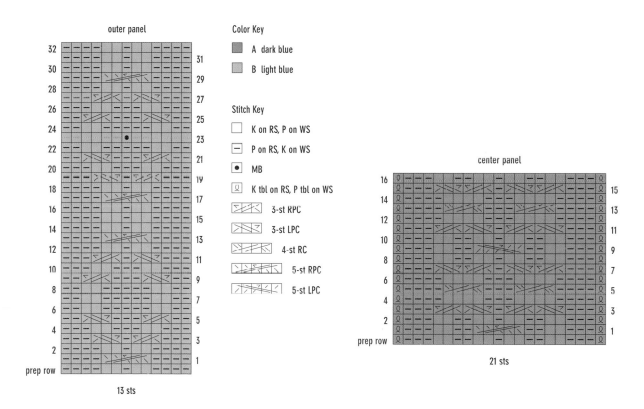

outer panel

Color Key

■ A dark blue

□ B light blue

Stitch Key

□ K on RS, P on WS

— P on RS, K on WS

• MB

Q K tbl on RS, P tbl on WS

3-st RPC

3-st LPC

4-st RC

5-st RPC

5-st LPC

center panel

13 sts

21 sts

133

4-st RC With A, sl 2 sts to cn and hold to back, k2, k2 from cn.

4-st LC With A sl 2 sts to cn and hold to front, k2, k2 from cn.

9-st LPC With A sl 5 sts to cn and hold to front, k4], with B p last st on cn, with A k4 from cn.

12-st RC With A sl 8 sts to cn and hold to back, k4, k last 4 sts from cn, k first 4 sts from cn.

12-st LC With A sl 8 sts to cn and hold to front, k4, k last 4 sts from cn, k first 4 sts from cn.

(begin with 37 sts)

Row 1 (RS) [P2 B, k4 A] 3 times, p1 B, [k4 A, p2 B] 3 times.

Row 2 and all WS rows With B, k the knit sts and m1 sts; with A, p the purl sts.

Row 3 P2 B, k4 A, p2 B, 4-st LC, p2 B, k4 A, p1 B, k4 A, p2 B, 4-st RC, p2 B, k4 A, p2 B.

Row 5 [P2 B, k4 A] 3 times, p1 B, [k4 A, p2 B] 3 times.

Row 7 P2 B, k4 A, p2 B, 4-st LC, p2 B, 9-st LPC, p2 B, 4-st RC, p2 B, k4 A, p2 B.

Row 9 P2 B, m1 B, [k4 A, p2B] twice, k4 A, m1 B, p1 B, m1 B, [k4 A, p2 B] twice, k4 A, m1 B, p2 B— 41 sts.

**Color Key**

☐ A white

▨ B blue

**Stitch Key**

☐ K on RS, P on WS

⊟ P on RS, K on WS

▱ 4-st RC

▱ 4-st LC

m make one

◿ P2tog

◿ P3tog

◸ Ssk

▱ 12-st RC

▱ 12-st LC

▱ 9-st LPC

▨ no stitch

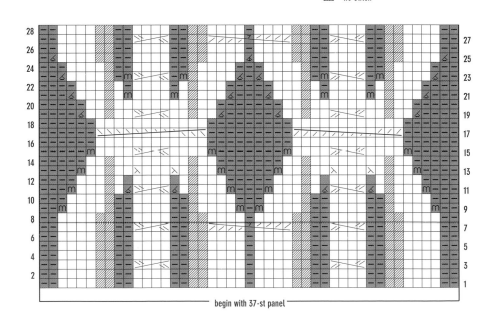

begin with 37-st panel

Row 11 P3 B, m1 B, k4 A, p2 B tog, 4-st LC, p2 B tog, k4 A, m1 B, p3 B, m1 B, k4 A, p2 B tog, 4-st RC, p2 B tog, k4 A, m1 B, p3 B.

Row 13 P4 B, m1 B, [k3 A, ssk A]twice, k4 A, m1 B, p5 B, m1 B, [k3 A, ssk A] twice, k4 A, m1 B, p4 B.

Row 15 P5 B, m1 B, k4 A, 4-st LC, k4 A, m1 B, p7 B, m1 B, k4 A, 4-st RC, k4 A, m1 B, p5 B — 45 sts.

Row 17 P6 B, 12-st LC, p9 B, 12-st RC, p6 B.

Row 19 P4 B, p2 B tog, k4 A, 4-st LC, k4 A, p2 B tog, p5 B, p2 B tog, k4 A, 4-st RC, k4 A, p2 B tog, p4 B—41sts.

Row 21 P3 B, p2 B tog, [k4 A, m1 B] twice, k4 A, p2 B tog, p3 B, p2 B tog, [k4 A, m1 B] twice, k4 A, p2 B tog, p3 B.

Row 23 P2 B, p2 B tog, k4 A, m1 B, p1 B, 4-st LC, m1 B, p1 B, k4 A, p2 B tog, p1 B, p2 B tog, k4 A, m1 B, p1 B, 4-st RC, m1 B, p1 B, k4 A, p2 B tog, p2 B.

Row 25 P1 B, p2 B tog, [k4 A, p2 B] twice, k4 A, p3 B tog, [k4 A, p2 B] twice, k4 A, p2 B tog, p1 B—37 sts.

Row 27 P2 B, k4 A, p2 B, 4-st LC, p2 B, 9-st LPC, p2 B, 4-st RC, p2 B, k4 A, p2 B.

Row 28 With B, k the knit sts and the m1 sts, with A, p the purl sts.

Rep rows 1–28.

A (light blue)

B (white)

(multiple of 20 sts plus 10)

Two-color X Sl 5 sts from holder to dpn. From RS with B, work in St st for 14 rows, place sts on holder. With A, work next 5 sts from safety pin in same way. Twist A and B strands and sl all 10 sts back to dpn.

Row 1 (RS) With A, knit.

Row 2 With A, k5, *sl 10 sts to safety pin or small st holder, hold to back of work, with separate bobbin of A cast 10 sts onto LH needle, keeping bobbin on RS of work. K tog sts on holder with cast on sts as follows: insert LH needle into back

of first st on holder (leave sts on holder) and k tog with first cast-on st on LH needle, then rep with rem 9 sts on holder and 9 cast-on sts (this closes up the opening between the holder and cast-on sts, leaving 10 sts on holder to be worked later), k10; rep from *, end k5.

Rows 3–16 With A, knit sts on needle, leaving holders to RS of work. Work Two-Color X s across row.

Row 17 With A, k5, *insert RH needle into back of first st on dpn and k tog with next st on LH needle, then rep with rem 9 sts on dpn and 9 sts on LH needle (this combines two-color x sts with LH needle sts), k10; rep from *, end k5. Cut extra yarn from Two-Color X s and fasten off.

Rows 18 and 19 With A, knit.

Row 20 With A, k15, work from * of row 2; end k15.

Rows 21–34 With A, knit sts on needle, leaving holders to RS of work. Work Two-Color X s across row.

Row 35 With A, k15, *insert RH needle into back of first st on dpn and k tog with next st on LH needle, then rep with rem 9 sts on dpn and 9 sts on LH needle (this combines Two-Color X sts with LH needle sts), k10; rep from *, end k15. Cut extra yarn from Two-Color X's and fasten off.

Row 36 With A, knit.

Rep rows 1–36.

(multiple of 16 sts)

Rows 1, 5, 9 and 13 (RS) *K1 B, p3 A; rep from * to end.

Row 2 *[P1 B, k3 A] 3 times, [p1 B, k1 A] twice; rep from * to end.

Rows 3, 7, 11 and 15 P2 A, *k1 B, p3 A; rep from *, end k1 B, p1 A.

Row 4 *P1 B, k1 A, [p1 B, k3 A] twice, p1 B, k1 A, p1 B, k3 A; rep from * to end.

Row 6 *K2A, [p1 B, k1 A, p1 B, k3 A] twice, p1 B, k1 A; rep from * to end.

Row 8 *P1 B, k3 A, [p1 B, k1 A] twice; [p1 B, k3 A] twice; rep from * to end.

Row 10 *K2 A, p1 B, k3, [p1 B, k1 A] twice, p1 B, k3 A, p1 B, k1 A; rep from * to end.

Row 12 *P1 B, k3 A, [p1 B, k1 A, p1 B, k3 A] twice; rep from * to end.

Row 14 *K2 A, p1 B, k1 A, [p1 B, k3 A] twice, [p1 B, k1 A] twice; rep from * to end.

Row 16 *P1 B, k1 A, [p1 B, k3 A] 3 times, p1 B, k1 A; rep from * to end.

Rep rows 1–16.

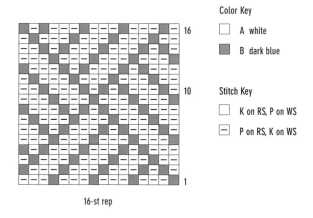

**Color Key**

A white

B dark blue

**Stitch Key**

K on RS, P on WS

P on RS, K on WS

16-st rep

# 155 tricolor cable

Note When crossing multicolored cables, keep colors in sequence as established. Use separate bobbins for each color in cable panel.

6-st RC Sl 3 sts to cn and hold to back of work, k3, k3 from cn.
6-st LC Sl 3 sts to cn and hold to front of work, k3, k3 from cn.
(worked over 21 sts)

Row 1 (RS) K3 A, k3 B, k3 C, p3 MC, k3 C, k3 B, k3 A.
Row 2 and 4 P3 A, p3 B, p3 C, k3 MC, p3 C, p3 B, p3 A.
Row 3 K3 A, k3 B, k3 C, p3 MC, k3 C, k3 B, k3 A.
Row 5 6-st RC, k3 C, p3 MC, k3 C, 6-st LC.
Rows 6 and 8 P3 B, p3 A, p3 C, k3 MC, p3 C, p3 A, p3 B.
Row 7 K3 B, k3 A, k3 C, p3 MC, k3 C, k3 A, k3 B.
Row 9 K3 B, 6-st LC, p3 MC, 6-st RC, k3 B.

Rows 10 and 12 P3 B, p3 C, p3 A, k3 MC, p3 A, p3 C, p3 B.
Row 11 K3 B, k3 C, k3 A, p3 MC, k3 A, k3 C, k3 B.
Row 13 6-st RC, k3 A, p3 MC, k3 A, 6-st LC.
Rows 14 and 16 P3 C, p3 B, p3 A, k3 MC, p3 A, p3 B, p3 C.
Row 15 K3 C, k3 B, k3 A, p3 MC, k3 A, k3 B, k3 C.
Row 17 K3 C; 6-st LC, p3 MC, 6-st RC, k3 C.
Rows 18 and 20 P3 C, p3 A, p3 B, k3 MC, p3 B, p3 A, p3 C.
Row 19 K3 C, k3 A, k3 B, p3 MC, k3 B, k3 A, k3 C.
Row 21 6-st RC, k3 B, p3 MC, k3 B; 6-st LC.
Rows 22 and 24 P3 A, p3 C, p3 B, k3 MC, p3 B, p3 C, p3 A.
Row 23 K3 A, k3 C, k3 B, p3 MC, k3 B, k3 C, k3 A.
Row 25 K3 A; 6-st LC, p3 MC; 6-st RC, k3 A.
Row 26 P3 A, p3 B, p3 C, k3 MC, p3 C, p3 B, p3 A.
Rep rows 3–26.

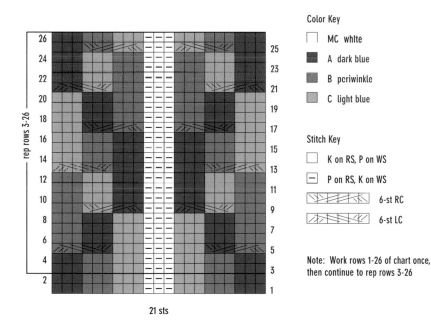

**Color Key**

☐ MC white
■ A dark blue
▨ B periwinkle
▨ C light blue

**Stitch Key**

☐ K on RS, P on WS
⊟ P on RS, K on WS

▨▨▨ 6-st RC

▨▨▨ 6-st LC

Note: Work rows 1-26 of chart once, then continue to rep rows 3-26

21 sts

rep rows 3-26

Note When crossing multicolored cables, keep colors in sequence as established.

Use separate bobbins for each color in cable panel.

6-st RC Sl 3 sts onto cn and hold to back of work, k3, k3 from cn.

6-st LC Sl 3 sts onto cn and hold to front of work, k3, k3 from cn.

(multiple of 16 sts)

Row 1 (RS) *P7 B, k3 B, k3 A, k3 C; rep from * to end.

Row 2 *P3 C, p3 A, p3 B, k7 B; rep from * to end.

Row 3 *P7 B, 6-st LC, k3 C; rep from * to end.

Rows 4 and 6 *P3 C, p3 B, p3 A, k7 B; rep from * to end.

Row 5 *P7 B, k3 A, k3 B, k3 C; rep from * to end.

Row 7 *P7 B, k3 A, 6-st RC; rep from * to end.

Row 8 *P3 B, p3 C, p3 A, k7 B; rep from * to end.

Row 9 *P7 A, k3 A, k3 C, k3 B; rep from * to end.

Row 10 *P3 B, p3 C, p3 A, k7 A; rep from * to end.

Row 11 *P7 A, 6-st LC, k3 B; rep from * to end.

Rows 12 and 14 *P3 B, p3 A, p3 C, k7 A; rep from * to end.

Row 13 *P7 A, k3 C, k3 A, k3 B; rep from * to end.

Row 15 *P7 A, k3 C, 6-st RC; rep from * to end.

Row 16 *P3 A, p3 B, p3 C, k7 A; rep from * to end.

Row 17 *P7 C, k3 C, k3 B, k3 A; rep from * to end.

Row 18 *P3 A, p3 B, p3 C, k7 C; rep from * to end.

Row 19 *P7 C, 6-st LC, k3 A; rep from * to end.

Rows 20 and 22 *P3 A, p3 C, p3 B, k7 C; rep from * to end.

Row 21 *P7 C, k3 B, k3 C, k3 A; rep from * to end.

Row 23 *P7 C, k3 B, 6-st RC; rep from * to end.

Row 24 *P3 C, p3 A, p3 B, k7 C; rep from * to end.

Rep rows 1–24.

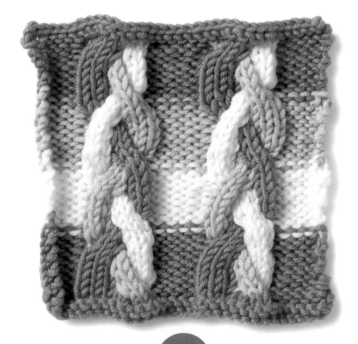

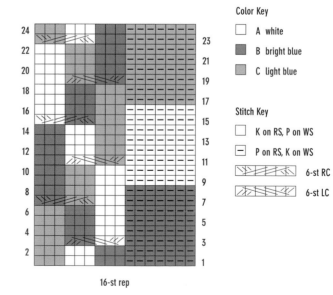

**Color Key**

☐ A white

■ B bright blue

■ C light blue

**Stitch Key**

☐ K on RS, P on WS

— P on RS, K on WS

6-st RC

6-st LC

16-st rep

156

Notes When crossing multicolored cables, keep colors in sequence as established.

Use separate bobbins for each color in cable panel.

6-st LC Slip 3 sts onto cn and hold to front of work, k3, k3 from cn.

(multiple of 13 sts plus 6 sts)

Row 1 (RS) *K6 A, k3 B, k1 A, k3 B; rep from *, end k6 A.

Rows 2 and 12 P6 A, *p2 B, p3 A, p2 B, p6 A; rep from * to end.

Rows 3 and 11 *K6 A, k1 B, k2 A, k1 B, k2 A, k1 B; rep from *, end k6 A.

Rows 4, 6, 8 and 10 P6 A, *p1 B, p1 A, p3 B, p1 A, p1 B, p6 A; rep from * to end.

Rows 5 and 9 *6-st LC, [k1 B, k1 A] 3 times, k1 B; rep from *, end 6-st LC.

Row 7 *K6 A, k1 B, k1 A, k3 B, k1 A, k1 B; rep from *, end k6 A.

Row 13 *K6 A, k3 B, k1 A, k3 B; rep from *, end k6 A.

Row 14 P6 A, *p1 B, p1 A, p3 B, p1 A, p1 B, p6 A; rep from * to end.

Row 15 *K6 A, [k1 B, k2 A] twice, k1 B; rep from *, end k6 A.

Row 16 P6 A, *p1 B, p1 A, p3 B, p1 A, p1 B, p6 A; rep from * to end.

Rep rows 1–16.

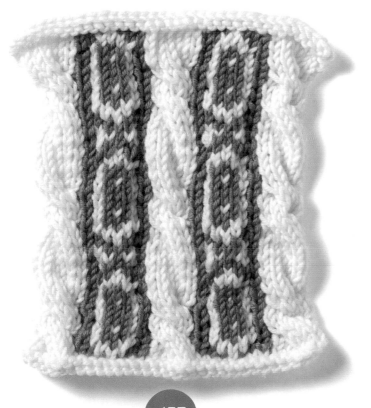

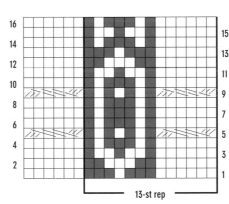

13-st rep

**Color Key**

☐ A  white

■ B  bright blue

**Stitch Key**

☐ K on RS, P on WS

▱ 6-st LC

**Note** When crossing multicolored cables, keep colors in sequence as established.

Use separate bobbins for each color in cable panel.

**3-st RPC** Sl 1 st onto cn and hold to back of work, k2, p1 from cn.

**3-st LPC** Sl 2 sts onto cn and hold to front of work, p1, k2 from cn.

**4-st RPC** Sl 2 sts onto cn and hold to back of work, k2, p2 from cn.

**4-st LPC** Sl 2 sts onto cn and hold to front of work, p2, k2 from cn.

**4-st RC** Sl 2 sts onto cn and hold to back of work, k2, k2 from cn.

**4-st LC** Sl 2 sts onto cn and hold to front of work, k2, k2 from cn.

(worked over 28 sts)

**Row 1 (RS)** P2 MC, k2 A, k2 B, k2 C, p12 MC, k2 C, k2 B, k2 A, p2 MC.

**Row 2** K2 MC, p2 A, p2 B, p2 C, k12 MC, p2 C, p2 B, p2 A, k2 MC.

**Row 3** P2 MC, k2 A, k2 B, 4-st LPC, p8 MC, 4-st RPC, k2 B, k2 A, p2 MC.

**Row 4** K2 MC, p2 A, p2 B, k2 MC, p2 C, k8 MC, p2 C, k2 MC, p2 B, p2 A, k2 MC.

**Row 5** P2 MC, k2 A, k2 B, p2 MC, 4-st LPC, p4 MC, 4-st RPC, p2 MC, k2 B, k2 A, p2 MC.

**Row 6** K2 MC, p2 A, p2 B, k4 MC, p2 C, k4 MC, p2 C, k4 MC, p2 B, p2 A, k2 MC.

**Row 7** P2 MC, k2 A, k2 B, p4 MC, 4-st LPC, 4-st RPC, p4 MC, k2 B, k2 A, p2 MC.

**Row 8** K2 MC, p2 A, p2 B, k6 MC, p4 C, k6 MC, p2 B, p2 A, k2 MC.

**Row 9** P2 MC, k2 A, 3-st LPC, p5 MC, 4-st RC, p5 MC, 3-st RPC, k2 A, p2 MC.

**Row 10** K2 MC, p2 A, k1 MC, p2 B, k5 MC, p4 C, k5 MC, p2 B, k1 MC, p2 A, k2 MC.

**Row 11** P2 MC, k2 A, p1 MC, 3-st LPC, p4 MC, k4 C, p4 MC, 3-st RPC, p1 MC, k2 A, p2 MC.

**Row 12** K2 MC, p2 A, k2 MC, p2 B, k4 MC, p4 C, k4 MC, p2 B, k2 MC, p2 A, k2 MC.

**Row 13** P2 MC, k2 A, p2 MC, 3-st LPC, p3 MC, 4-st RC, p3 MC, 3-st RPC, p2 MC, k2 A, p2 MC.

**Row 14** K2 MC, p2 A, k3 MC, p2 B, k3 A, p4 C, k3 MC, p2 B, k3 MC, p2 A, k2 MC.

**Row 15** P2 MC, k2 A, p3 MC, 3-st LPC, 4-st RPC, 4-st LPC, 3-st RPC, p3 MC, k2 A, p2 MC.

**Row 16** K2 MC, p2 A, k4 MC, p2 B, p2 C, k4 MC, p2 C, p2 B, k4 MC, p2 A, k2 MC.

**Row 17** P2 MC, k2 A, p4 MC, 4-st LC, p4 MC, 4-st LC, p4 MC, k2 A, p2 MC.

**Row 18** K2 MC, p2 A, k4 MC, p2 C, p2 B, k4 MC, p2 B, p2 C, k4 MC, p2 A, k2 MC.

**Row 19** P2 MC, 3-st LPC, p2 MC, 3-st RPC, 4-st LPC, 4-st RPC, 3-st LPC, p2 MC, 3-st RPC, p2 MC.

**Row 20** K3 MC, p2 A, k2 MC, p2 C, k3 MC, p4 B, k3 MC, p2 C, k2 MC, p2 A, k3 MC.

**Row 21** P3 MC, 3-st LPC, 3-st RPC, p3 MC, 4-st RC, p3 MC, 3-st LPC, 3-st RPC, p3 MC.

**Row 22** K4 MC, p2 A, p2 C, k4 MC, p4 B, k4 MC, p2 C, p2 A, k4 MC.

**Row 23** P4 MC, 4-st RC, p4 MC, k4 B, p4 MC, 4-st RC, p4 MC.

**Row 24** K4 MC, p2 C, p2 A, k4 MC, p4 B, k4 MC, p2 A, p2 C, k4 MC.

**Row 25** P3 MC, 3-st RPC, 3-st LPC, p3 MC, 4-st RC, p3 MC, 3-st RPC, 3-st LPC, p3 MC.

**Row 26** K3 MC, p2 C, k2 MC, p2 A, k3 MC, p4 B, k3 MC, p2 A, k2 MC, p2 C, k3 MC.

**Row 27** P2 MC, 3-st RPC, p2 MC, 3-st LPC, 4-st RPC, 4-st LPC, 3-st RPC, p2 MC, 3-st LPC, p2 MC.

**Row 28** K2 MC, p2 C, k4 MC, p2 A, p2 B, k4 MC, p2 B, p2 A, k4 MC, p2 C, k2 MC.

**Row 29** P2 MC, k2 C, p4 MC, 4-st LC, p4 MC, 4-st LC, p4 MC, k2 C, p2 MC.

**Row 30** K2 MC, p2 C, k4 MC, p2 B, p2 A, k4 MC, p2 A, p2 B, k4 MC, p2 C, k2 MC.

**Row 31** P2 MC, k2 C, p3 MC, 3-st RPC,

4-st LPC, 4-st RPC, 3-st LPC, p3 MC, k2 C, p2 MC.

Row 32 K2 MC, p2 C, k3 MC, p2 B, k3 MC, p4 A, k3 MC, p2 B, k3 MC, p2 C, k2 MC.

Row 33 P2 MC, k2 C, p2 MC, 3-st RPC, p3 MC, 4-st RC, p3 MC, 3-st LPC, p2 MC, k2 C, p2 MC.

Row 34 K2 MC, p2 C, k2 MC, p2 B, k4 MC, p4 A, k4 MC, p2 B, k2 MC, p2 C, k2 MC.

Row 35 P2 MC, k2 C, p1 MC, 3-st RPC, p4 MC, k4 A, p4 MC, 3-st LPC, p1 MC, k2 C, p2 MC.

Row 36 K2 MC, p2 C, k1 MC, p2 B, k5 MC, p4 A, k5 MC, p2 B, k1 MC, p2 C, k2 MC.

Row 37 P2 MC, k2 C, 3-st RPC, p5 MC, 4-st RC, p5 MC, 3-st LPC, k2 C, p2 MC..

Row 38 K2 MC, p2 C, p2 B, k6 MC, p4 A, k6 MC, p2 B, p2 C, k2 MC.

Row 39 P2 MC, k2 C, k2 B, p4 MC, 4-st RPC, 4-st LPC, p4 MC, k2 B, k2 C, p2 MC.

Row 40 K2 MC, p2 C, p2 B, k4 MC, p2 A, k4 MC, p2 A, k4 MC, p2 B, p2 C, k2 MC.

Row 41 P2 MC, k2 C, k2 B, p2 MC, 4-st RPC, p4 MC, 4-st LPC, p2 MC, k2 B, k2 C, p2 MC.

Row 42 K2 MC, p2 C, p2 B, k2 MC, p2 A, k8 MC, p2 A, k2 MC, p2 B, p2 C, k2 MC.

Row 43 P2 MC, k2 C, k2 B, 4-st RPC, p8 MC, 4-st LPC, k2 B, k2 C, p2 MC.

Rows 44 and 46 K2 MC, p2 C, p2 B, p2 A, k12 MC, p2 A, p2 B, p2 C, k2 MC.

Rows 45 and 47 P2 MC, k2 C, k2 B, k2 A, p12 MC, k2 A, k2 B, k2 C, p2 MC.

Row 48 K2 MC, p2 C, p2 B, p2 A, k12 MC, p2 A, p2 B, p2 C, k2 MC.

Rep rows 1–48, cont in color pat as est, second repeat of this pattern will begin with different color sequence than first repeat.

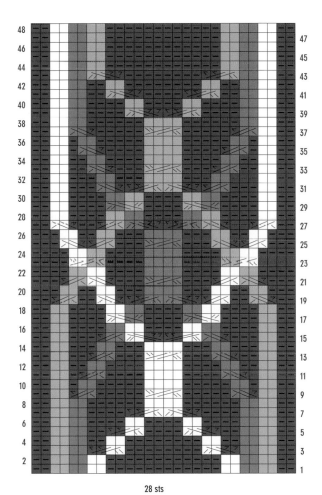

28 sts

**Color Key**

■ MC dark blue

■ A pale blue

■ B periwinkle

□ C white

**Stitch Key**

□ K on RS, P on WS

— P on RS, K on WS

 3-st- RPC

3-st LPC

4-st RPC

4-st LPC

4-st RC

4-st LC

# 159 bicolor cable

(multiple of 15 sts plus 12)

Notes When crossing multicolored cables, keep colors in sequence as established.

Use separate bobbins for each color in cable panel.

8-st RC Slip 4 sts to cn and hold to back of work, [k1 B, k1 A] twice, [k1 B, k1 A] twice from cn.

Row 1 (RS) *P2 A, [k1 B, k1 A] 4 times, p2 A, k3 A; rep from *, end p2 A, [k1 B, k1 A] 4 times, p2 A.

Rows 2, 4, 6, 8 K2 A, [p1 A, p1 B] 4 times, k2 A, *p3 A, k2 A, [p1 A, p1 B] 4 times, k2 A; rep from * to end.

Rows 3, 5 and 7 *P2 A, [k1 B, k1 A] 4 times, p2 A, k3 A; rep from *, end p2 A, [k1 B, k1 A] 4 times, p2 A.

Row 9 *P2 A, 8-st RC, p2 A, k3 A; rep from *, end p2 A, 8-st RC, p2 A.

Row 10 K2 A, [p1 A, p1 B] 4 times, k2 A, *p3 A, k2 A, [p1 A, p1 B] 4 times, k2 A; rep from * to end.

Rep rows 3–10.

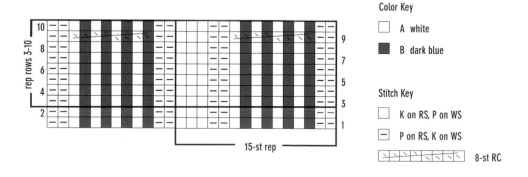

**Color Key**

☐ A white

■ B dark blue

**Stitch Key**

☐ K on RS, P on WS

— P on RS, K on WS

8-st RC

15-st rep

rep rows 3-10

Note When crossing multicolored cables, keep colors in sequence as established. Use separate bobbins for each color in cable panel.

8-st RC Sl 4 sts to cn and hold to back, k4, k4 from cn.

8-st LC Sl 4 sts to cn and hold to front, k4, k4 from cn.

8-st RCA Sl 4 sts to cn and hold to back, with A, k4, with B, k4 from cn.

8-st RCB Sl 4 sts to cn and hold to back, with B, k4, with A, k4 from cn.

8-st LCA Sl 4 sts to cn and hold to front, with B, k4, with A, k4 from cn.

8-st LCB Sl 4 sts to cn and hold to front, with A, k4, with B, k4 from cn.

(multiple of 18 sts)

Row 1 (RS) *P1 A, k8 A; rep from * to end.

Row 2 *P8 A, k1 A; rep from * to end.

Row 3 *P1 A, k8 A, p1 A, 8-st RCA; rep from * to end.

Rows 4 and 6 *P4 B, p4 A, k1 A, p8 A, k1 A; rep from * to end.

Row 5 *P1 A, k8 A, p1 A, k4 A, k4 B; rep from * to end.

Row 7 *P1 A, k8 A, p1 A, 8-st RCB; rep from * to end.

Row 8 *P4 A, p4 B, k1 A, p8 A, k1 A; rep from * to end.

Row 9 *P1 A, k8 A; rep from * to end.

Rows 10, 12 and 14 *P8 A, k1 A; rep from * to end.

Row 11 *P1 A, k8 A, p1 A, 8-st RC; rep from * to end.

Row 13 *P1 A, k8 A; rep from * to end.

Row 15 *P1 A, 8-st LCA, p1 A, k8 A; rep from * to end.

Rows 16 and 18 *P8 A, k1 A, p4 A, p4 B, k1 A; rep from * to end.

Row 17 *P1 A, k4 B, k4 A, p1 A, k8 A; rep from * to end.

Row 19 *P1 A, 8-st LCB, p1 A, k8 A; rep from * to end.

Row 20 *P8 A, k1 A, p4 B, p4 A, k1 A; rep from * to end.

Row 21 *P1 A, k8 A; rep from * to end.

Row 22 *P8 A, k1 A; rep from * to end.

Row 23 *P1 A, 8-st LC, p1 A, k8 A; rep from * to end.

Row 24 *P8 A, k1 A; rep from * to end.

Rep rows 1–24.

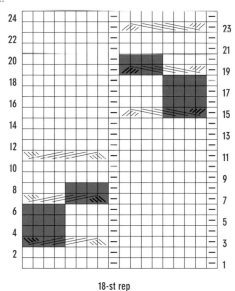

**Color Key**

☐ A white

■ B bright blue

**Stitch Key**

☐ K on RS, P on WS

— P on RS, K on WS

8-st RCA

8-st RCB

8-st RC

8-st LCA

8-st LCB

8-st LC

18-st rep

# 161 blues 'round midnight

Note When crossing multicolored cables, keep colors in sequence as established.

Use separate bobbins for each color in cable panel.

12-st RC Sl 6 sts to cn and hold to back, k6, k6 from cn.

12-st LC Sl 6 sts to cn and hold to front, k6, k6 from cn. (worked over 30 sts)

Preparation row (WS) P6 B, p6 A, p6 B, p6 A, p6 B.

Rows 1, 3, 5, 7, 9, 11 (RS) K6 B, k6 A, p6 B, k6 A, k6 B.

Rows 2, 4, 6, 8, 10, 12 P6 B, p6 A, k6 B, p6 A, p6 B.

Row 13 12-st RC, p6 B, 12-st LC.

Row 14 P6 A, p6 B, p6 A, p6 B, p6 A.

Rows 15, 17, 19, 21, 23 and 25 K6 A, k6 B, p6 A, k6 B, k6 A.

Rows 16, 18, 20, 22, 24 and 26 P6 A, p6 B, k6 A, p6 B, p6 A.

Row 27 12-st RC, p6 A, 12-st LC.

Row 28 P6 B, p6 A, p6 B, p6 A, p6 B.

Rep rows 1–28.

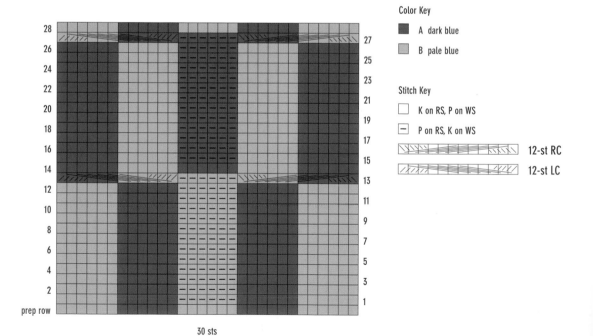

**Color Key**

■ A  dark blue

■ B  pale blue

**Stitch Key**

☐ K on RS, P on WS

— P on RS, K on WS

12-st RC

12-st LC

30 sts

## 162 rosebud trellis

A (pale blue)

B (periwinkle)

MB (make bobble) *K next st on LH needle, do not sl off needle. Sl new st from RH needle to LH needle. Working into new st each time, rep from * 4 times more—5 sts from 1 st. K6, then pass the 2nd, 3rd, 4th, 5th and 6th st over first st on RH needle.

(multiple of 6 sts plus 7)

Cast on with A.

Preparation row (WS) With A, purl.

Row 1 (RS) With B, k1, wyif sl 2, *MB, wyif sl 5, rep from *, end MB, wyif sl 2, k1.

Row 2 With B, p1, wyib sl 2, *p1, wyib sl 5; rep from *, end p1, wyib sl 2, p1.

Rows 3 and 5 With A, knit.

Rows 4, 6 and 8 With A, purl.

Row 7 With A, k5, *insert RH needle from front under top loose B strand and k next st, hooking strand behind st as it's knit; in same way, insert RH needle under both B strands and k next st, then under top B strand again and k next st, k3; rep from *, end k2.

Row 9 With B, k1, *wyif sl 5, MB; rep from *, end wyib sl 5, k1.

Row 10 With B, p1, *wyib sl 5, p1; rep from *, end wyib sl 5, p1.

Rows 11–14 With A, rep rows 3–6.

Row 15 With A, k2, *insert RH needle from front under top loose B strand and k next st, hooking strand behind st as it's knit; in same way, insert RH needle under both B strands and k next st, then under top B strand again and k next st, k3; rep from *, end k2.

Row 16 With A, purl.

Rep rows 1–16.

162

(multiple of 5 sts plus 1)

A (bright blue)

B (light blue)

**Cross 4** Drop long st on LH needle and let hang in front of work. Sl next 2 sts to RH needle. Drop 2nd long st. Insert LH needle into first dropped st, sl 2 sts on RH needle back to LH needle and insert LH needle into 2nd dropped st, k4.

Cast on with A.

**Preparation row (WS)** With A, purl.

**Row 1 (RS)** With A, knit.

**Row 2** With A, p1, *p1 wrap yarn twice around needle, p2, p1 wrap yarn twice around needle, p1; rep from * to end.

**Row 3** With B, k1, *wyib sl 1 and drop extra wrap, k2, wyib sl 1 and drop extra wrap, (k1, yo, k1, yo, k1) all in next st; rep from *, end wyib sl 1 and drop extra wrap, k2, wyib sl 1 and drop extra wrap, k1.

**Row 4** With B, p1, *wyif sl 1, p2, wyif sl 1, k5; rep from *, end wyif sl 1, p2, wyif sl 1, p1.

**Row 5** With B, k1, *wyib sl 1, k2, wyib sl 1, p5; rep from *, end wyib sl 1, k2, wyib sl 1, k1.

**Row 6** With B, p1, *wyif sl 1, p2, wyif sl 1, k2tog, k3tog, pass the 2nd st over first st on RH needle; rep from *, end wyif sl 1, p2, wyif sl 1, p1.

**Row 7** With A, k1, *Cross 4, k1; rep from * to end.

**Row 8** With A, p1, *p4, k1; rep from *, end p5.

**Rows 9–10** With B, rep rows 1–2.

**Rows 11–14** With A, rep rows 3–6.

**Rows 15–16** With B, rep rows 7–8.

Rep rows 1–16.

163

## 164 reversible 4-color brioche

(over an odd number of sts)

A (light blue)

B (white)

C (dark blue)

D (pale blue)

**Sl 1 yo** Lay the yarn under the needle to front of the work, and slip the following stitch purlwise. Then lay the yarn over the needle and over the slipped stitch to the back.

**Sl 1 yof** Leaving the yarn in front, slip the following stitch purlwise. Lay the yarn over the needle and over the slipped stitch, and then under the needle to the front.

With A, cast on an odd number of sts on circular needle.

**Row 1 (RS)** With A, k1, *sl 1 yo, k1; rep from *, end sl 1 yo, k1.

**Row 2 (WS)** With B, k1, *k2tog, sl 1 yo; rep from *, end k2tog, k1.

**Row 3 (RS)** With C, k1, *sl 1 yo, k2tog; rep from *, end sl 1 yo, k1.

**Row 4 (WS)** With D, rep row 2. Do not turn. Slide sts to other end of needle.

**Row 5 (WS)** With A, k1, *sl 1 yof, p2tog; rep from *, end sl 1 yof, k1.

**Row 6 (RS)** With B, k1, *p2tog, sl 1 yof; rep from *, end p2tog, k1.

**Row 7 (WS)** With C, rep row 5.

**Row 8 (RS)** With D, rep row 6. Do not turn. Slide sts to other end of needle.

**Row 9 (RS)** With A, rep row 3.

Rep rows 2–9.

# adding texture

## 165 2-color brioche rib

A (bright blue)

B (light blue)

Sl 1 yo Lay the yarn under the needle to front of the work, and slip the following stitch purl-wise. Then lay the yarn over the needle and over the slipped stitch to the back.

Sl 1 yof Leaving the yarn in front, slip the following stitch purlwise. Lay the yarn over the needle and over the slipped stitch, and then under the needle to the front.

(over an odd number of sts)

Cast on with A.

Row 1 (RS) With A, k1, *sl 1 yo, k1; rep from *, end sl 1 yo, k1.

Rows 2 and 6 (WS) With B, k1, *k2tog, sl 1 yo; rep from *, end k2tog, k1. Do not turn. Slide sts back to opposite end of needle.

Row 3 (WS) With A, k1, *sl 1 yof, p2tog; rep from *, end sl 1 yo, k1.

Row 4 (RS) With B, k1, *p2tog, sl 1 yof; rep from *, end p2tog, k1. Do not turn. Slide sts back to opposite end of needle.

Row 5 (RS) With A, k1, *sl 1 yo, k2tog; rep from *, end with sl 1 yo, k1.

Row 7 (WS) With A, k1, *sl 1 yof, p2tog; rep from *, end sl 1 yo, k1.

Row 8 (RS) With B, k1, *p2tog, sl 1 yof; rep from *, end p2tog, k1. Do not turn.  Slide sts back to opposite end of needle.

Rows 9 and 13 (RS) With A, k1, *sl 1 yof, p2tog; rep from *, end sl 1 yo, k1.

Rows 10 and 14 (WS) With B, k1, *p2tog, sl 1 yof; rep from *, end p2tog, k1. Do not turn. Slide sts back to opposite end of needle.

Rows 11 and 15 (WS) With A, k1, *sl 1 yo, k2tog; rep from *, end sl 1 yo, k1.

Rows 12 and 16 (RS) With B, k1, *k2tog, sl 1 yo; rep from *, end k2tog, k1. Do not turn. Slide sts to back opposite end of needle.

Row 17 (RS) With A, k1, *sl 1 yo, k2tog; rep from *, end with sl 1 yo, k1.

Rep rows 2–17.

165

## 166 knotty

A (dark blue)

B (pale blue)

Bows are picked up and knit from existing garter st fabric.

With A, knit garter st swatch.

*With B, pick up 5 sts along one garter ridge.

Work 5-st strip in St st for 2½"/6.5cm.

Bind off.

Work a second strip directly above the first with 4 garter ridges between.

Tie lower and upper strips in square knot as follows: wrap lower over upper and then tie right over left to complete knot.

Rep from * as desired on swatch.

## 167 when doves cry

Tweed st Insert needle into next st 2 rows below and pull up loop, k next st on LH needle, pass loop over that st.

(multiple of 4 sts plus 3)

Prep row (WS) With B, purl.

Row 1 With A, *k3, Tweed st; rep from *, end k3.

Rows 2 With A, purl.

Rows 3 With B, *k1, Tweed st, k2; rep from *, end k1, Tweed st, k1.

Rows 4 With B, purl.

Rep rows 1–4.

# adding texture

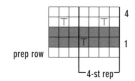

Color Key

A periwinkle

B white

Stitch Key

T Tweed St

K on RS, P on WS

166

167

A (periwinkle)

B (pale blue)

**Note** Pat is worked back and forth in rows on double pointed or circular needles.

**Sl 1 yo** Lay the yarn under the needle to front of the work and slip the following stitch purlwise. Then lay the yarn over the needle and over the slipped stitch to the back.

**Sl 1 yof** Leaving the yarn in front, slip the following stitch purlwise. Lay the yarn over the needle and over the slipped stitch, and then under the needle to the front.

(multiple of 2 sts)

**Row 1 (WS)** With A, k1, *k1, sl 1 yo; rep from *, end k1. Do not turn. Slide sts back to opposite end of needle.

**Row 2 (WS)** With B, k1, *k2tog, sl 1 yo; rep from *, end k1.

**Row 3 (RS)** With A, k1, *k2tog, sl 1 yo; rep from *, end k1. Do not turn. Slide sts back to opposite end of needle.

**Row 4 (RS)** With B, k1, *sl 1 yof, p2tog; rep from *, end k1.

**Row 5 (WS)** With A, k1, *sl 1 yof, p2tog; rep from *, end k1. Do not turn. Slide sts back to opposite end of needle.

**Row 6 (WS)** With B, rep row 3.

Rep rows 3–6.

slip stitch

## 169 peas and carrots

(multiple of 4 sts plus 2)
Row 1 (WS) With MC, purl.
Row 2 With A, k1, wyib sl 1, *k2, wyib sl 2; rep from *, end k2, wyib sl 1, k1.
Row 3 With A, p1, wyif sl 1, p2, *wyif sl 2, p2; rep from *, end wyif sl 1, p1.
Row 4 With MC, knit.
Row 5 With B, *p2, wyif sl 2; rep from *, end p2.
Row 6 With B, k2, *wyib sl 2, k2; rep from * to end.
Rep rows 1–6.

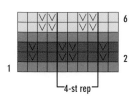

**Color Key**
- ■ MC peach
- ■ A orange
- ☐ B medium green

**Stitch Key**
- ☐ K on RS, P on WS
- Ⅴ wyib sl 1 on RS, wyif sl 1 on WS

169

## 170 tumbleweeds

(multiple of 2 sts plus 1)
Row 1 (RS) With A, k1, *wyif sl 1, k1; rep from * to end.
Row 2 With A, purl.
Row 3 With MC, k1, *k1, wyif sl 1; rep from *, end k2.
Row 4 With MC, purl.
Row 5 With MC, knit.
Row 6 With MC, purl.
Rep rows 1–6.

**Color Key**
- ■ MC rust
- ■ A peach

**Stitch Key**
- ☐ K on RS, P on WS
- Ⅴ wyif sl 1 on RS, wyib sl 1 on WS

170

# 171 painted desert

(multiple of 2 sts)

**Note** Pattern is worked back and forth in rows on dpn or circular needle.

**Row 1 (WS)** With F, *wyif sl 1, p1; rep from * to end.

**Rows 2 and 4** With F, knit.

**Row 3** With F, purl.

**Row 5** With F, *wyib sl 1, p1; rep from * to end.

**Row 6** With C, *wyif sl 1, wyib sl 1; rep from * to end.

**Row 7** With D, *wyib sl 1, p1; rep from * to end.

**Row 8** With D, knit.

**Row 9** With E, purl. Do not turn. Slide sts back to opposite end of needle.

**Row 10 (WS)** With A, *wyib sl 1, wyif sl 1; rep from * to end. Do not turn. Slide sts back to opposite end of needle.

**Row 11 (WS)** With D, *p1, wyib sl 1; rep from * to end.

**Row 12** With D, knit.

**Row 13** With D, purl. Do not turn. Slide sts back to opposite end of needle.

**Row 14 (WS)** With C, *wyif sl 1, wyib sl 1; rep from * to end.

**Row 15** With F, *k1, wyif sl 1; rep from * to end.

**Row 16** With F, purl.

**Row 17** With F, knit. Do not turn. Slide sts back to opposite end of needle.

**Row 18 (RS)** With A, *wyib sl 1, k1; rep from * to end.

**Row 19** With A, purl.

**Row 20** With A, knit. Do not turn. Slide sts back to opposite end of needle.

**Row 21 (RS)** With E, *wyif sl 1, wyib sl 1; rep from * to end.

**Row 22** With B, *p1, wyif sl 1; rep from * to end.

**Row 23** With B, knit.

**Row 24** With B, purl.

**Row 25** With D, *k1, wyib sl 1; rep from * to end.

**Row 26** With D, *wyif sl 1, p1; rep from * to end.

**Row 27** With B, knit.

**Row 28** With B, purl. Do not turn. Slide sts back to opposite end of needle.

**Row 29 (WS)** With A, *wyif sl 1, p1; rep from * to end.

**Row 30** With A, knit.

**Row 31** With E, *wyif sl 1, wyib sl 1; rep from * to end. Do not turn. Slide sts back to opposite end of needle.

**Row 32 (WS)** With A, purl. Do not turn. Slide sts back to opposite end of needle.

Rep rows 1–32.

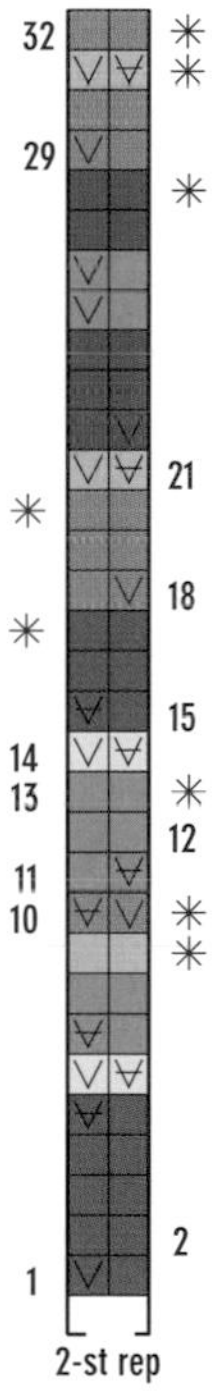


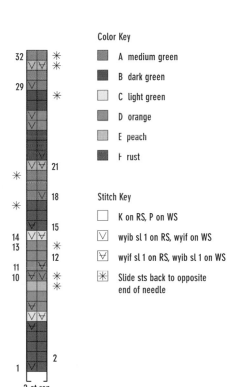

**Color Key**

- A medium green
- B dark green
- C light green
- D orange
- E peach
- F rust

**Stitch Key**

- K on RS, P on WS
- wyib sl 1 on RS, wyif on WS
- wyif sl 1 on RS, wyib sl 1 on WS
- Slide sts back to opposite end of needle

171

(multiple of 6 sts plus 5)

Row 1 (RS) With MC, knit.

Row 2 With MC, purl.

Row 3 With A, k2, *wyib sl 1, k1; rep from *, end  wyib sl 1, k2.

Row 4 With A, k2, wyif sl 1, *k1, wyif sl 1, p1, wyif sl 1, k1, wyif sl 1; rep from *, end k2.

Rows 5 and 7 With MC, k2, *k3, wyib sl 1, k2; rep from * , end k3.

Rows 6 and 8 With MC, p3, *p2, wyif sl 1, p3; rep from *, end p2.

Row 9 With MC, knit.

Row 10 With MC, purl.

Row 11 With B, *k1, wyib sl 1; rep from *, end k1.

Row 12 With B, k1, wyif sl 1, p1, *[wyif sl 1, k1] twice , wyif sl 1, p1; rep from *, end wyif sl 1, k1.

Rows 13 and 15 With MC, k2, *wyib sl 1, k5; rep from *, end wyib sl 1, k2.

Rows 14 and 16 With MC, p2, wyif sl 1, *p5, wyif sl 1; rep from *, end p2.

Rep rows 1–16.

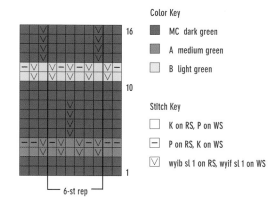

**Color Key**

■ MC  dark green

■ A  medium green

□ B  light green

**Stitch Key**

□ K on RS, P on WS

– P on RS, K on WS

∨ wyib sl 1 on RS, wyif sl 1 on WS

6-st rep

# 173 bargello

(multiple of 4 sts plus 5)

ML (make loop) Insert RH needle into the next st 2 rows below and pull up a loose loop of yarn, k the next st, pass the loop over the st just knit.

Preparation Row 1 (WS) With MC, purl.

Preparation Row 2 With MC, knit.

Preparation Row 3 With MC, p2, p1 wrapping yarn around needle twice, *p3, p1 wrapping yarn around needle twice; rep from *, end p2.

Row 1 (RS) With A, k2, *wyib sl 1 dropping extra wrap, k1, ML, k1; rep from *, end wyib sl 1 dropping extra wrap, k2.

Row 2 With A, p2, wyif sl 1, *p3, wyif sl 1; rep from *, end p2.

Row 3 With A, knit.

Row 4 With A, p2, p1 wrapping yarn around needle twice, *p3, p1 wrapping yarn around needle twice; rep from *, end p2.

Rows 5–8 With MC, rep rows 1–4.

Rows 9–12 With B, rep rows 1–4.

Rows 13–16 With MC, rep rows 1–4.

Rows 17–20 With C, rep rows 1–4.

Rows 21–24 With MC, rep rows 1–4.

Rep rows 1–24.

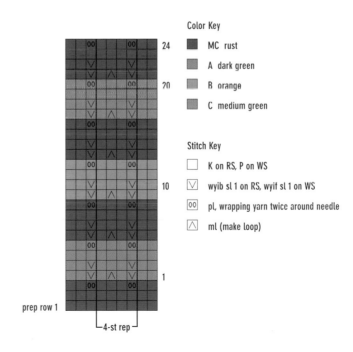

**Color Key**

■ MC  rust

■ A  dark green

■ B  orange

■ C  medium green

**Stitch Key**

☐ K on RS, P on WS

∨ wyib sl 1 on RS, wyif sl 1 on WS

00 p1, wrapping yarn twice around needle

∧ ml (make loop)

prep row 1

└ 4-st rep ┘

173

(multiple of 4 sts)

Rows 1, 3, 5 and 7 (RS) With MC, knit.

Rows 2, 4, 6 and 8 With MC, purl.

Row 9 With A, k1, *wyib sl 2, wyif sl 2; rep from *, end wyib sl 2, k1.

Row 10 With A, p1, wyif sl 2, *wyib sl 2, wyif sl 2; rep from *, end p1.

Rows 11 and 13 With MC, knit.

Rows 12 and 14 With MC, purl.

Row 15 With A, k1, *wyib sl 2, wyif sl 2; rep from *, end wyib sl 2, k1.

Row 16 With A, p1, wyif sl 2, *wyib sl 2, wyif sl 2; rep from *, end p1.

Rows 17, 19, 21 and 23 With MC, knit.

Rows 18, 20, 22 and 24 With MC, purl.

Row 25 With B, k1, *wyib sl 2, wyif sl 2; rep from *, end wyib sl 2, k1.

Row 26 With B, p1, wyif sl 2, *wyib sl 2, wyif sl 2; rep from *, end p1.

Rows 27 and 29 With MC, knit.

Rows 28 and 30 With MC, purl.

Row 31 With B, k1, *wyib sl 2, wyif sl 2; rep from *, end wyib sl 2, k1.

Row 32 With B, p1, wyif sl 2, * wyib sl 2, wyif sl 2; rep from *, end p1.

Rep rows 1–32.

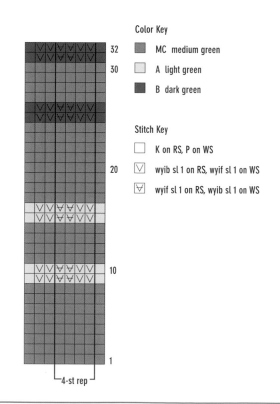

**Color Key**

■ MC medium green

□ A light green

■ B dark green

**Stitch Key**

□ K on RS, P on WS

∨ wyib sl 1 on RS, wyif sl 1 on WS

⋏ wyif sl 1 on RS, wyib sl 1 on WS

4-st rep

## 175 garter grid

(multiple of 3 sts)
Row 1 (RS) With B, *wyib sl 1, k2;
rep from * to end.
Row 2 With B, knit.
Row 3 With A, *k2, wyib sl 1;
rep from * to end.
Row 4 With A, knit.
Rep rows 1–4.

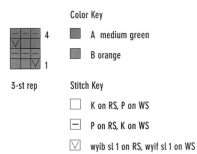

3-st rep

**Color Key**

■ A medium green

■ B orange

**Stitch Key**

☐ K on RS, P on WS

— P on RS, K on WS

⊻ wyib sl 1 on RS, wyif sl 1 on WS

175

## 176 grid

(multiple of 2 sts)
Row 1 (RS) With B, k1, *k1, wyif sl 1;  rep from *, end k1.
Row 2 With B, k1, *wyif sl 1, k1; rep from *, end k1.
Row 3 With A, k1, *wyif sl 1, k1; rep from *, end k1.
Row 4 With A, k1, *k1, wyif sl 1; rep from *, end k1.
Rep rows 1–4.

# slip stitch

2-st rep

**Color Key**

☐ A light green

■ B medium green

**Stitch Key**

☐ K on RS, P on WS

— P on RS, K on WS

⊻ wyib sl 1 on RS, wyif sl 1 on WS

⋈ wyif sl 1 on RS, wyib sl 1 on WS

176

# 177 plaid

(multiple of 10 sts plus 2)

MC (dark green)

A (peach)

Note Pattern is worked back and forth in rows on dpn or circular needle.

Rows 1, 5 and 9 (RS) With A, k1, *[wyif sl 1, wyib sl 1] twice, wyif sl 1, k5; rep from *, end k1. Do not turn. Slide sts to opposite end of needle.

Rows 2 and 6 (RS) With MC, k1, *k5, wyib sl 5; rep from *, end k1.

Rows 3 and 7 (WS) With A, k1, *p5, [wyif sl 1, wyib sl 1] twice, wyif sl 1; rep from *, end k1. Do not turn. Slide sts to opposite end of needle.

Rows 4 and 8 (WS) With MC, k1, *wyif sl 5, p5; rep from *, end k1.

Rows 10, 14, and 18 (RS) With MC, k1, *k5, [wyif sl 1, wyib sl 1] twice, wyif sl 1; rep from *, end k1.

Rows 11 and 15 (WS) With A, k1, *p5, wyif sl 5; rep from *, end k1. Do not turn. Slide sts to opposite end of needle.

Rows 12 and 16 (WS) With MC, k1, *[wyif sl 1, wyib sl 1] twice, wyif sl 1, p5; rep from *, end k1.

Rows 13 and 17 (RS) With A, k1, *wyib sl 5, k5; rep from *, end k1. Do not turn. Slide sts to opposite end of needle.

Rows 19, 23 and 27 (WS) With A, k1, *p5, [wyib sl 1, wyif sl 1] twice, wyib sl 1; rep from *, end k1. Do not turn. Slide sts to opposite end of needle.

Rows 20 and 24 (WS) With MC, k1, *wyif sl 5, p5; rep from *, end k1.

Rows 21 and 25 (RS) With A, k1, *[wyib sl 1, wyif sl 1] twice, wyib sl 1, k5; rep from *, end k1. Do not turn. Slide sts to opposite end of needle.

Rows 22 and 26 (RS) With MC, k1, *k5, wyib sl 5; rep from *, end k1.

Rows 28 and 32 (WS) With MC, k1, [wyib sl 1, wyif sl 1] twice, wyib sl 1, p5; rep from *, end k1.

Rows 29 and 33 (RS) With A, k1, *wyib sl 5, k5; rep from *, end k1. Do not turn. Slide sts to opposite end of needle.

Rows 30 and 34 (RS) With MC, k1, *k5, [wyib sl 1, wyif sl 1] twice, wyib sl 1; rep from *, end k1.

Rows 31 and 35 (WS) With A, k1, *p5, wyif sl 5; rep from *, end k1. Do not turn. Slide sts to opposite end of needle.

Row 36 (WS) With MC, k1, [wyib sl 1, wyif sl 1] twice, wyib sl 1, p5; rep from *, end k1.

Rep rows 1–36.

177

# 178 masonry

(multiple of 4 sts plus 3)

Rows 1, 2, 5 and 6 With MC, knit.

Row 3 (RS) With A, k1, *wyib sl 1, k3; rep from *, end wyib sl 1, k1.

Row 4 With A, p1, wyif sl 1, *p3, wyif sl 1; rep from *, end p1.

Row 7 With A, k1, *k2, wyib sl 1, k1; rep from *, end k2.

Row 8 With A, p2, *p1, wyif sl 1, p2; rep from *, end p1.

Rep rows 1–8.

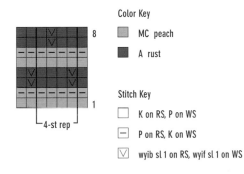

**Color Key**

🟦 MC  peach

🟪 A  rust

**Stitch Key**

☐ K on RS, P on WS

▬ P on RS, K on WS

▽ wyib sl 1 on RS, wyif sl 1 on WS

# 179 sicilian pie

(multiple of 9 sts plus 4)

Row 1 (RS) With MC, knit.

Row 2 With MC, purl.

Rows 3 and 7 With A, k1, *wyib sl 2, k1, [wyif sl 1, k1] 3 times; rep from *, end wyib sl 2, k1.

Rows 4 and 8 With A, p1, wyif sl 2, *p7, wyif sl 2; rep from *, end p1.

Rows 5 and 9 With MC, k1, *k1, [k1, wyif sl 1] 4 times, k2; rep from *, end k3.

Row 6 With MC, purl.

Row 10 With MC, purl.

Rep rows 1–10.

## slip stitch

**Color Key**

🟦 MC medium green

🟪 A orange

**Stitch Key**

☐ K on RS, P on WS

▽ wyib sl 1 on RS, wyif sl 1 on WS

⋏ wyif sl 1 on RS, wyib sl 1 on WS

178

179

## 180 spring planting

(multiple of 10 sts plus 11)

Note Pattern is worked back and forth in rows on dpn or circular needle.

Row 1 (RS) With B, wyib sl 1, k1, *k5, wyif sl 2, k3; rep from *, end k2.

Row 2 With B, wyib sl 1, k1, wyib sl 2, k3, p2, *k3, wyib sl 2, k3, p2; rep from *, end k2. Do not turn. Slide sts back to opposite end of needle.

Row 3 (WS) With A, wyib sl 1, k6, wyif sl 2, *k8, wyif sl 2; rep from *, end k2.

Row 4 With A, wyib sl 1, k1, *wyib sl 2, k3, p2, k3; rep from *, end k2. Do not turn. Slide sts back to opposite end of needle.

Rep rows 1–4.

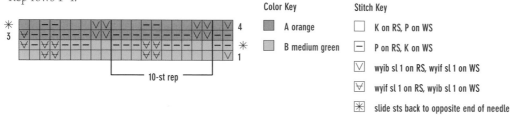

**Color Key**

■ A orange

■ B medium green

**Stitch Key**

☐ K on RS, P on WS

− P on RS, K on WS

∨ wyib sl 1 on RS, wyif sl 1 on WS

⅄ wyif sl 1 on RS, wyib sl 1 on WS

✳ slide sts back to opposite end of needle

## 181 tiny brocade

(multiple of 4 sts plus 3)

Rows 1 and 5 (WS) With MC, purl.

Row 2 With A, k1, wyif sl 1, k1, *wyib sl 1, k1, wyif sl 1, k1; rep from * to end.

Row 3 With A, *p3, wyif sl 1; rep from *, end p3.

Row 4 With MC, k1, wyif sl 1, k1, *k2, wyif sl 1, k1; rep from * to end.

Row 6 With A, k1, wyib sl 1, k1, *wyif sl 1, k1, wyib sl 1, k1; rep from * to end.

Row 7 With A, *p1, wyif sl 1, p2; rep from *, end p1, wyif sl 1, p1.

Row 8 With MC, k3, *wyib sl 1, k3; rep from * to end.

Rep rows 1–8.

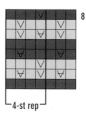

**Color Key**

■ MC dark green

■ A light green

**Stitch Key**

☐ K on RS, P on WS

∨ wyib sl 1 on RS, wyif sl 1 on WS

⅄ wyif sl 1 on RS, wyib sl 1 on WS

## 182 little bricks

(multiple of 8 sts plus 2)

Note Pattern is worked back and forth in rows on dpn or circular needle.

Row 1 (RS) With C, knit. Do not turn. Slide sts to opposite end of needle.

Row 2 (RS) With A, k1, *k7, wyib sl 1; rep from *, end k1.

Row 3 (WS) With A, p1, *wyif sl 1, k7; rep from *, end p1.

Row 4 With A, k1, *p7, wyib sl 1; rep from *, end k1.

Row 5 With A, p1, *wyif sl 1, k7; rep from *, end p1. Do not turn. Slide sts to opposite end of needle.

Row 6 (WS) With C, purl.

Row 7 With B, k1, *k3, wyib sl 1, k4; rep from *, end k1.

Row 8 With B, p1, *k4, wyif sl 1, k3; rep from *, end p1.

Row 9 With B, k1, *p3, wyib sl 1, p4; rep from *, end k1.

Row 10 With B, p1, *k4, wyif sl 1, k3; rep from *, end p1.

Rep rows 1–10.

## 183 striped rib

(multiple of 2 sts)

Row 1 (RS) With A, *k1, wyib sl 1; rep from * to end.

Row 2 With A, *k1, wyif sl 1; rep from * to end.

Row 3 With MC, *k1, wyib sl 1; rep from * to end.

Row 4 With MC, *k1, wyif sl 1; rep from * to end.

Rep rows 1–4.

**Color Key**

- ▣ MC orange
- ▣ A medium green

**Stitch Key**

- ☐ K on RS, P on WS
- — P on RS, K on WS
- ☑ wyib sl 1 on RS, wyif sl 1 on WS

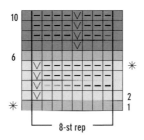

8-st rep

**Color Key**

- ☐ A light green
- ▣ B orange
- ▣ C peach

**Stitch Key**

- ☐ K on RS, P on WS
- — K on WS, P on RS
- ☑ wyib sl 1 on RS, wyif sl 1 on WS
- ✳ slide sts back to opposite end of needle

182

183

# 184 cluster quilting

(multiple of 8 sts plus 1)

MC (medium green)

A (peach)

**Wrap 3** Pick up first dropped A st and knit it, k1, pick up next dropped A st and knit it, [wyib, sl last 3 sts worked to LH needle, pass yarn to front, sl same 3 sts back to RH needle, pass yarn to back] twice.

**Preparation row (WS)** With A, p1, *p1 wrapping yarn twice around needle, p5, p1 wrapping yarn twice around needle, p1; rep from * to end.

**Row 1 (RS)** With MC, k1, *wyib sl 1 dropping extra wrap, k5, wyib sl 1 dropping extra wrap, k1; rep from * to end.

**Row 2** With MC, *p1, wyif sl 1, p5, wyif sl; rep from *, end p1.

**Row 3** With MC, k1, *wyib sl 1, k5, wyib sl 1, k1; rep from * to end.

**Row 4** With MC, purl, dropping all elongated A sl sts off needle to RS of work.

**Row 5** With A, k1, *wyib sl 1, k1, wrap 3, k1, wyib sl 2; rep from *, end wyib sl 1, k1.

**Row 6** With A, p1, wyif sl 1, *[p1, p1 wrapping yarn twice around needle] twice, p1, wyif sl 3; rep from *, end wyif sl 1, p1.

**Row 7** With MC, k1, *k2, wyib sl 1 dropping extra wrap, k1, wyib sl 1 dropping extra wrap, k3; rep from * to end.

**Row 8** With MC, *p3, wyif sl 1, p1, wyif sl 1, p2; rep from *, end p1.

**Row 9** With MC, k1, *k2, wyib sl 1, k1, wyib sl 1, k3; rep from * to end.

**Row 10** With MC, purl, dropping all elongated A sl sts off needle to RS of work.

**Row 11** With A, k1, *pick up first dropped st and knit it, k1, wyib sl 3, k1, *wrap 3, k1, wyib sl 3, k1; rep from *, end pick up last dropped st and knit it, k1.

**Row 12** With A, p1, *p1 wrapping yarn twice around needle, p1, wyif sl 3, p1, p1 wrapping yarn twice around needle, p1; rep from * to end.

Rep rows 1–12.

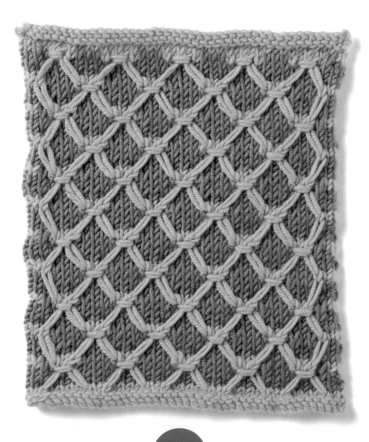

184

# 185 honeycomb

(multiple of 6 sts plus 3)

MC (orange)

A (peach)

**Preparation row (RS)** With A, knit.

**Row 1 (WS)** With A, knit.

**Row 2** With MC, k4, *wyib sl 1, k5, turn; wyif sl 1, p4, turn; wyib sl 1, k4, turn; wyif sl 1, p4; then wyif sl 1, wyib sl 1; bring yarn through to WS, then sl last 2 sts back again to LH needle, turn; wyib sl 1, k4; rep from *, end wyib sl 1, k4.

**Row 3** With MC, p4, *wyif sl 1, p5; rep from *, end wyif sl 1, p4.

**Row 4** With A, k4, *k1tbl, k5; rep from *, end k1tbl, k4.

**Row 5** With A, knit.

**Row 6** With MC, k1, *wyib sl 1, k5, turn; wyif sl 1, p4, turn; wyib sl 1, k4, turn; wyif sl 1, p4; then wyif sl 1, wyib sl 1; bring yarn through to WS, then sl last 2 sts back again to LH needle, turn; wyib sl 1, k4; rep from *, end wyib sl 1, k1.

**Row 7** With MC, p1, *wyif sl 1, p5; rep from *, end wyif sl 1, p1.

**Row 8** With A, k1, *k1tbl, k5; rep from *, end k1tbl, k1.

Rep rows 1–8.

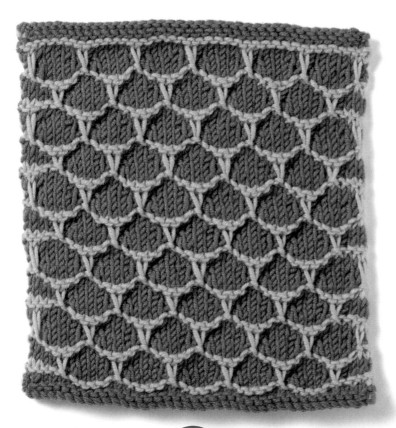

185

# 186 radar

(multiple of 8 sts plus 1)

Note Pattern is worked back and forth in rows on dpn or circular needle.

3-st LPC RS rows Sl 1 st to cn and hold to front, p2, k1 from cn.

WS rows Sl 2 sts to cn and hold to front, p1, k2 from cn.

3-st RPC RS rows Sl 2 sts to cn and hold to back, k1, p2 from cn.

WS rows Sl 1 st to cn and hold to back, k2, p1 from cn.

Preparation row (RS) With MC, *k1, p3; rep from *, end k1. Do not turn. Slide sts back to opposite end of needle.

Row 1 (RS) With A, *wyib sl 1, p3; rep from *, end wyib sl 1.

Row 2 (WS) With MC, k1, *k1, 3-st LPC; rep from * to end. Do not turn. Slide sts back to opposite end of needle.

Row 3 (WS) With B, *k2, wyif sl 1, k1; rep from *, end k1.

Row 4 (RS) With MC, p1, *p1, 3-st LPC; rep from * to end. Do not turn. Slide sts back to opposite end of needle.

Row 5 (RS) With C, *wyib sl 1, p3; rep from *, end wyib sl 1.

Row 6 (WS) With MC, k1, *k1, 3-st LPC; rep from * to end. Do not turn. Slide sts back to opposite end of needle.

Row 7 (WS) With A, *k2, wyif sl 1, k1; rep from *, end k1.

Row 8 (RS) With MC, p1, *p1, 3-st LPC; rep from * to end. Do not turn. Slide sts back to opposite end of needle.

Row 9 (RS) With B, *wyib sl 1, p3; rep from *, end wyib sl 1.

Row 10 (WS) With MC, k1, *k1, 3-st LPC; rep from * to end. Do not turn. Slide sts back to opposite end of needle.

Row 11 (WS) With C, *k2, wyif sl 1, k1; rep from *, end k1.

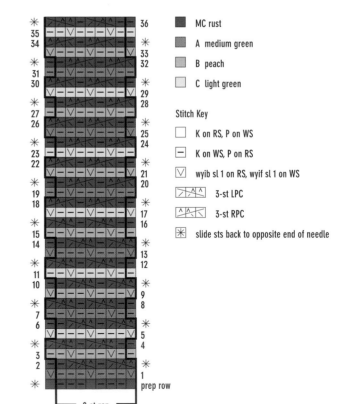

MC rust

A medium green

B peach

C light green

Stitch Key

☐ K on RS, P on WS

━ K on WS, P on RS

∨ wyib sl 1 on RS, wyif sl 1 on WS

3-st LPC

3-st RPC

✳ slide sts back to opposite end of needle

8-st rep

186

Row 12 (RS) With MC, p1, *p1, 3-st LPC;
rep from * to end. Do not turn. Slide sts back to opposite end of needle.

Row 13 (RS) With A, *wyib sl 1, p3; rep from *, end p1.

Row 14 (WS) With MC, k1, *k1, 3-st LPC;
rep from * to end. Do not turn. Slide sts back to opposite end of needle.

Row 15 (WS) With B, *k2, wyif sl 1, k1; rep from *, end k1.

Row 16 (RS) With MC, p1, *p1, 3-st LPC;
rep from * to end. Do not turn. Slide sts back to opposite end of needle.

Row 17 (RS) With C, wyib sl 1, *p3, wyib sl 1; rep from * to end.

Row 18 (WS) With MC, *3-st RPC, k1; rep from *, end k1. Do not turn.
Slide sts back to opposite end of needle.

Row 19 (WS) With A, k1, *k1, wyif sl 1, k2; rep from *, to end.

Row 20 (RS) With MC, *3-st RPC, p1; rep from *, end p1. Do not turn.
Slide sts back to opposite end of needle.

Row 21 (RS) With B, wyib sl 1, *p3, wyib sl 1; rep from  to end.

Row 22 (WS) With MC, *3-st RPC, k1; rep from *; end k1. Do not turn.
Slide sts back to opposite end of needle.

Row 23 (WS) With C, k1, *k1, wyif sl 1, k2; rep from * to end.

Row 24 (RS) With MC, *3-st RPC, p1; rep from *, end p1. Do not turn.
Slide sts back to opposite end of needle.

Row 25 (RS) With A, wyib sl 1, *p3, wyib sl 1; rep from * to end.

Row 26 (WS) With MC, *3-st RPC, k1; rep from *, end k1.
Sl sts back to other end of needle.

Row 27 (WS) With B, k1, *k1, wyif sl 1, k2; rep from * to end.

Row 28 (RS) With MC, *3-st RPC, p1; rep from *, end p1. Do not turn.
Slide sts back to opposite end of needle.

Row 29 (RS) With C, wyib sl 1, *p3, wyib sl 1; rep from to end.

Row 30 (WS) With MC, *3-st RPC, k1; rep from *; end k1. Do not turn.
Slide sts back to opposite end of needle.

Row 31 (WS) With A, k1, *k1, wyif sl 1, k2; rep from * to end.

Row 32 (RS) With MC, *3-st RPC, p1; rep from *, end p1. Do not turn.
Slide sts back to opposite end of needle.

Row 33 (RS) With B, wyib sl 1, *p3, wyib sl 1; rep from to end.

Row 34 (WS) With MC, *3-st RPC, k1; rep from *; end k1. Do not turn.
Slide sts back to opposite end of needle.

Row 35 (WS) With C, *k2, wyif sl 1, k1; rep from *, end k1.

Row 36 (RS) With MC, p1, *p1, 3-st LPC; rep from * to end. Do not turn.
Slide sts back to opposite end of needle.

Rep rows 1–36.

(multiple of 11 sts plus 2)

6-st SC Sl 2 sts to cn and hold to back of work, k1, k1 from cn, wyib sl 2nd st from cn to RH needle, sl next st to cn and hold to front of work, wyib sl next st, k1, k st from cn.

Prep row 1 (RS) With B, knit.

Prep row 2 With B, purl.

Prep row 3 With A, *k5, wyib sl 2, k4; rep from *, end k2.

Prep row 4 With A, p2, *p4, wyif sl 2, p5; rep from * to end.

Row 1 (RS) With B, *k3, 6-st SC, k2; rep from *, end k2.

Row 2 With B, p2, *p4, wyif sl 2, p5; rep from * to end.

Row 3 With A, *k3, 6-st SC, k2; rep from *, end k2.

Row 4 With A, p2, *p4, wyif sl 2, p5; rep from * to end.

Rep rows 1–4.

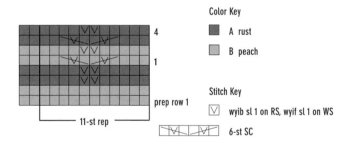

**Color Key**

■ A rust

■ B peach

**Stitch Key**

☑ wyib sl 1 on RS, wyif sl 1 on WS

6-st SC

11-st rep

prep row 1

(begin with a multiple of 8 sts plus 3)

Row 1 (RS) With MC, knit.

Row 2 With MC, purl.

Row 3 With A, *wyib sl 3, k1, wyib sl 3, [k1, yo, k1, yo, k1, yo, k1] into next st; rep from *, end wyib sl 3.

Row 4 With A, sl 3 wyif, *k7, wyif sl 3, k1, wyif sl 3 ; rep from * to end.

Row 5 With MC, k1, *k5, k2tog, k5, ssk; rep from *, end k2.

Row 6 With MC, p2, *p2tog, p1, wyif sl 1, p1, p2tog, p5; rep from *, end p1.

Row 7 With MC, k1, *k5, k2tog, wyib sl 1, ssk; rep from *, end k2.

Rows 8 and 10 With MC, purl.

Row 9 With MC, knit.

Row 11 With B, *wyib sl 3, [k1, yo, k1, yo, k1, yo, k1] into next st, wyib sl 3, k1; rep from *, end wyib sl 3.

Row 12 With B, wyif sl 3, *k1, wyif sl 3, k7, wyif sl 3, rep from * to end.

Row 13 With MC, *k2, k2tog, k5, ssk, k3; rep from *, end k3.

Row 14 With MC, p3, *p3, p2tog, p1, wyif sl 1, p1, p2tog, p2; rep from * to end.

Row 15 With MC, *k2, k2tog, wyib sl 1, ssk, k3; rep from *, end k3.

Row 16 With MC, purl.

Rep rows 1–16.

## 189 diamond brocade

(multiple of 12 sts plus 3)

Row 1 (RS) With A, k1, *[k2, wyib sl 1] twice, [k1, wyib sl 1, k1] twice; rep from *, end k2.

Row 2 With A, k2, *[k1, wyif sl 1, k1] twice, [wyif sl 1, k2] twice; rep from *, end k1.

Row 3 With B, k1, *wyib sl 1, k2; rep from *, end wyib sl 1, k1.

Row 4 With B, k1, wyif sl 1, *k2, wyif sl 1; rep from *, end k1.

Row 5 With A, k1, *k1, wyib sl 1, k2, wyib sl 1, k3, wyib sl 1, k2, wyib sl 1; rep from *, end k2.

Row 6 With A, k2, *[wyif sl 1, k2] twice, [k1, wyif sl 1, k1] twice; rep from *, end k1.

Row 7 With B, k1, *[k2, wyif sl 1] twice, [k1, wyif sl 1, k1] twice; rep from *, end k2.

Row 8 With B, k2, *[k1, wyif sl 1, k1] twice, [wyif sl 1, k2] twice; rep from *, end k1.

Row 9 With A, k1, *wyib sl 1, k2; rep from *, end wyib sl 1, k1.

Row 10 With A, k1, wyif sl 1,  *k2, wyif sl 1; rep from *, end k1.

Row 11 With B, k1, *[k1, wyib sl 1, k1] twice, [k2, wyib sl 1] twice; rep from *, end k2.

Row 12 With B, k2, *[wyif sl 1, k2] twice, [k1, wyif sl 1, k1] twice; rep from *, end k1.

Row 13 With A, k1, *[k2, wyib sl 1] twice, [k1, wyib sl 1, k1] twice; rep from *, end k2.

Row 14 With A, k2, *[k1, wyif sl 1, k1] twice, [wyif sl 1, k2] twice; rep from *, end k1.

Row 15 With B, k1, *wyib sl 1, k2; rep from *, end wyib sl 1, k1.

Row 16 With B, k1, wyif sl 1, *k2, wyif sl 1; rep from *, end k1.

Row 17 With A, k1, *[k1, wyib sl 1, k1] twice, [k2, wyib sl 1] twice; rep from *, end k2.

Row 18 With A, k2, *[wyif sl 1, k2] twice, [k1, wyif sl 1, k1] twice; rep from *, end k1.

Row 19 With B, k1, *wyib sl 1, k2; rep from *, end wyib sl 1, k1.

Row 20 With B, k1, wyif sl 1, *k2, wyif sl 1; rep from *, end k1.

Row 21 With A, k1, *[k2, wyib sl 1] twice, [k1, wyib sl 1, k1] twice; rep from *, end k2.

Row 22 With A, k2, *[k1, wyif sl 1, k1] twice,  [wyif sl 1, k2] twice; rep from *, end k1.

Row 23 With B, k1, *[k1, wyib sl 1, k1] twice, [k2, wyib sl 1] twice; rep from *, end k2.

Row 24 With B, k2, *[wyif sl 1, k2] twice, [k1, wyif sl 1, k1] twice; rep from *, end k1.

Row 25 With A, k1, *wyib sl 1, k2; rep from *, end wyib sl 1, k1.

Row 26 With A, k1, wyif sl 1,  *k2, wyif sl 1; rep from *, end k1.

Row 27 With B, k1, *[k2, wyib sl 1] twice, [k1, wyib sl 1, k1] twice; rep from *, end k2.

Row 28 With B, k2, *[k1, wyif sl 1, k1] twice, [wyif sl 1, k2]; rep from *, end k1.

Row 29 With A, k1, *[k1, wyib sl 1, k1] twice, [k2, wyib sl 1]; rep from *, end k2.

Row 30 With A, k2, *[wyif sl 1, k2] twice, [k1, wyif sl 1, k1] twice; rep from *, end k1.

Row 31 With B, k1, *wyib sl 1, k2; rep from *, end wyib sl 1, k1.

Row 32 With B, k1, wyif sl 1, *k2, wyif sl 1; rep from *, end k1.

Rep rows 1–32.

189

**slip stitch**

(multiple of 6 sts plus 2)

Preparation row 1 (RS) With A, knit.

Preparation row 2 With A, p1, *wyib sl 3, p3; rep from *, end p1.

Preparation row 3 With B, knit.

Row 1 With B, p1, *p3, wyib sl 3 sts; rep from *, end p1.

Row 2 With A, k1, *k4, insert RH needle from front to back into horizontal A strand 3 rows below and k this strand tog with next B st on LH needle, k1; rep from *, end k1.

Row 3 With A, p1, *wyib sl 3, p3; rep from *, end p1.

Row 4 With B, k1, *k1, insert RH needle from front to back into horizontal B strand 3 rows below and k this strand tog with next A st on LH needle, k4; rep from *, end k1.

Rep rows 1–4.

**Color Key**

- A dark green
- B rust

**Stitch Key**

- ☐ K on RS, P on WS
- ⊟ P on RS, K on WS
- ☒ wyib sl 1 on RS, wyif sl 1 on WS

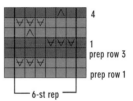

6-st rep

**Color Key**

- A orange
- B dark green

**Stitch Key**

- ☐ K on RS, P on WS
- ☒ wyif sl 1 on RS, wyib sl 1 on WS
- ◺ Insert RH needle from front to back into horizontal strand 3 rows below, k this strand tog with next st of opposite color on LH needle

190

(multiple of 8 sts plus 11)

Rows 1 and 9 (RS) With B, knit.

Rows 2 and 10 With B, knit.

Rows 3 and 7 With A, k3, *[wyib sl 1, k1] twice, wyib sl 1, k3; rep from * to end.

Rows 4 and 8 With A, *p3, [wyif sl 1, k1] twice, wyif sl 1; rep from *, end p3.

Row 5 With B, k1, wyib sl 2, *k5, wyib sl 3; rep from *, end k5, wyib sl 2, k1.

Row 6 With B, k1, wyif sl 2, k5, *wyif sl 3, k5; rep from *, end wyif sl 2, k1.

Rows 11 and 15 With A, [k1, wyib sl 1] twice, *k2, [k1, wyib sl 1] three times; rep from *, end k3, [wyib sl 1, k1] twice.

Row 12 With A, [k1, sl 1 wyif] twice, p3, *[wyif sl 1, k1] twice, wyif sl 1, p3; rep from *, end [wyif sl 1, k1] twice.

Row 13 With B, k4, *wyib sl 3, k5; rep from *, end wyib sl 3, k4.

Row 14 With B, k4, wyif sl 3, *k5, wyif sl 3; rep from *, end k4.

Row 16 With A, [k1, wyif sl 1] twice, p3, wyif sl 1, *[k1, wyif sl 1] twice, p3, wyif sl 1; rep from * end k1, wyif sl 1, k1.

Rep rows 1–16.

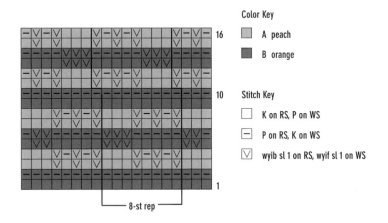

Color Key

A peach

B orange

Stitch Key

☐ K on RS, P on WS

─ P on RS, K on WS

☑ wyib sl 1 on RS, wyif sl 1 on WS

8-st rep

(multiple of 8 sts)

Row 1 (RS) With B, *k4, wyib sl 1, k3; rep from * to end.

Row 2 With B, *p3, wyif sl 1, p4; rep from * to end.

Row 3 With A, *k2, [k1, wyib sl 1] three times; rep from * to end.

Row 4 With A, *[wyif sl 1, p1] three times, p2; rep from * to end.

Row 5 With B, *[wyib sl 1, k1] three times, k2; rep from * to end.

Row 6 With B, *p2, [p1, wyif sl 1] three times; rep from * to end.

Row 7 With A, *k3, wyib sl 1, k4; rep from * to end.

Row 8 With A, *p4, wyif sl 1, p3; rep from * to end.

Row 9 With B, *wyib sl 1, k7; rep from * to end.

Row 10 With B, *p7, wyif sl 1; rep from * to end.

Row 11 With A, *[k1, wyib sl 1] twice, k3, wyib sl 1; rep from * to end.

Row 12 With A, *wyif sl 1, p3, [wyif sl 1, p1] twice; rep from * to end.

Row 13 With B, *wyib sl 1, k3, [wyib sl 1, k1] twice; rep from * to end.

Row 14 With B, *[p1, wyif sl 1] twice, p3, wyif sl 1; rep from * to end.

Row 15 With A, *k7, wyib sl 1; rep from * to end.

Row 16 With A, *wyif sl 1, p7; rep from * to end.

Rep rows 1–16.

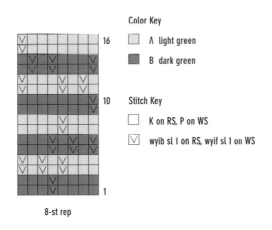

**Color Key**

∧ A light green

B dark green

**Stitch Key**

☐ K on RS, P on WS

∨ wyib sl 1 on RS, wyif sl 1 on WS

8-st rep

# 193 netting

(multiple of 2 sts)

Note Pattern is worked back and forth in rows on dpn or circular needle.

Preparation row (WS) With B, purl.

Row 1 (RS) With A, *k1, wyib sl 1; rep from * to end. Do not turn. Slide sts back to opposite end of needle.

Row 2 (RS) With B, *k1, wyib sl 1; rep from * to end.

Row 3 (WS) With A, *p1, wyif sl 1; rep from * to end. Do not turn. Slide sts back to opposite end of needle.

Row 4 (WS) With B, *p1, wyif sl 1; rep from * to end.

Rep rows 1–4.

2-st rep

Color Key

☐ A peach

■ B rust

Stitch Key

☐ K on RS, P on WS

Ⅴ wyib sl 1 on RS, wyif sl 1 on WS

✳ slide sts back to opposite end of needle

# 194 switching yard

(multiple of 14 sts)

Row 1 (RS) With B, *wyib sl 1, k5, [wyib sl 1, k3] twice; rep from * to end.

Row 2 With B, *[p3, wyif sl 1] twice, k5, wyif sl 1; rep from * to end.

Row 3 With A, *[k3, wyib sl 1] twice, k5, wyib sl 1; rep from * to end.

Row 4 With A, *wyif sl 1, k5, [wyif sl 1, p3] twice; rep from * to end.

Rep rows 1–4.

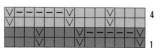

Color Key

☐ A peach

■ B orange

Stitch Key

☐ K on RS, P on WS

⊟ P on RS, K on WS

Ⅴ wyib sl 1 on RS, wyif sl 1 on WS

193

194

(multiple of 8 sts plus 3)

Row 1 (RS) With MC, knit.

Row 2 With MC, purl.

Row 3 With A, k2, *wyib sl 1, k5, wyib sl 1, k1; rep from *, end k1.

Row 4 With A, p1, *p1, wyif sl 1, p5, wyif sl 1; rep from *, end p2.

Rows 5 and 9 With MC, k2, *k1, wyib sl 1, k2; rep from *, end k1.

Rows 6 and 10 With MC, p1, *p2, wyif sl 1, p1; rep from *, end p2.

Row 7 With A, k2, *k2, wyib sl 1, k1, wyib sl 1, k3; rep from *, end k1.

Row 8 With A, p1, *p3, wyif sl 1, p1, wyif sl 1, p2; rep from *, end p2.

Row 11 With A, k2, *wyib sl 1, k5, wyib sl 1, k1; rep from *, end k1.

Row 12 With A, p1, *p1, wyif sl 1, p5, wyif sl 1; rep from *, end p2.

Row 13  With MC, knit.

Row 14 With MC, purl.

Rep rows 1–14.

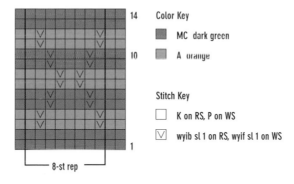

**Color Key**

MC  dark green

A  orange

**Stitch Key**

K on RS, P on WS

wyib sl 1 on RS, wyif sl 1 on WS

8-st rep

(multiple of 4 sts plus 3)

Row 1 (RS) With B, knit.

Row 2 With B, knit.

Row 3 With A, k3, *wyib sl 1, k3; rep from * to end.

Row 4 With A, *k3, wyif sl 1; rep from *, end k3.

Row 5 With B, k1, wyib sl 1, k1, *k2, wyib sl 1, k1; rep from * to end.

Row 6 With B, *k1, wyif sl 1, k2; rep from *, end k1, wyif sl 1, k1.

Row 7 With A, k2, wyib sl 1, *k1, wyib sl 1, k2; rep from * to end.

Row 8 With A, *k2, wyif sl 1, k1; rep from *, end wyif sl 1, k2.

Row 9 With B, k3, *wyib sl 1, k3; rep from * to end.

Row 10 With B, *k3, wyif sl 1; rep from *, end k3.

Row 11 With A, k1, wyib sl 1, k1, *k2, wyib sl 1, k1; rep from * to end.

Row 12 With A, *k1, wyif sl 1, k2; rep from *, end k1, wyib sl 1, k1.

Rows 13 and 14 With B, knit.

Row 15 With A, k1, wyib sl 1, k1, *k2, wyib sl 1, k1; rep from * to end.

Row 16 With A, *k1, wyif sl 1, k2; rep from *, end k1, wyib sl 1, k1.

Row 17 With B, k3, *wyib sl 1, k3; rep from * to end.

Row 18 With B, *k3, wyif sl 1; rep from *, end k3.

Row 19 With A, k2, wyib sl 1, * k1, wyib sl 1, k2; rep from * to end.

Row 20 With A, *k2, wyif sl 1, k1; rep from *, end wyif sl 1, k2.

Row 21 With B, k1, wyib sl 1, k1, *k2, wyib sl 1, k1; rep from * to end.

Row 22 With B, *k1, wyif sl 1, k2; rep from *, end k1, wyif sl 1, k1.

Row 23 With A, k3, *wyib sl 1, k3; rep from * to end.

Row 24 With A, *k3, wyif sl 1; rep from *, end k3.

Rows 25 and 26 With B, knit.

Rep rows 1–26.

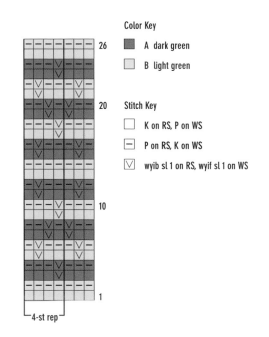

**Color Key**

■ A dark green

□ B light green

**Stitch Key**

□ K on RS, P on WS

— P on RS, K on WS

∨ wyib sl 1 on RS, wyif sl 1 on WS

4-st rep

# 197 double diamonds

(multiple of 20 sts plus 1)

Row 1 (RS) With A, *k5, wyib sl 1, k9, wyib sl 1, k4; rep from *, end k1.

Row 2 With A, p1, *p4, wyif sl 1, p9, wyif sl 1, p5; rep from * to end.

Row 3 With B, knit.

Row 4 With B, k1, *k3, p3, k7, p3, k4; rep from * to end.

Row 5 With A, *k4, wyib sl 1, k1, wyib sl 1, k3; rep from *, end k1.

Row 6 With A, p1, *p3, wyif sl 1, k1, wyif sl 1, p4; rep from * to end.

Row 7 With B, knit.

Row 8 With B, k1, *k2, p5, k5, p5, k3; rep from * to end.

Row 9 With A, *k3, [wyib sl 1, k1] three times, k1; rep from *, end k1.

Row 10 With A, p1, *p2, [wyif sl 1, k1] twice, wyif sl 1, p3; rep from * to end.

Row 11 With B, knit.

Row 12 With B, k1, *k1, p7, k3, p7, k2; rep from * to end.

Row 13 With A, *k2, [wyib sl 1, k1] four times; rep from *, end k1.

Row 14 With A, p1, *p1, [wyif sl 1, k1] three times, wyif sl 1, p2; rep from * to end.

Row 15 With B, knit.

Row 16 With B, purl.

Row 17 With A, *k1, wyib sl 1; rep from *, end k1.

Row 18 With A, k1, *wyif sl 1, k1; rep from * to end.

Row 19 With B, knit.

Row 20 With B, purl.

Row 21 With A, *k2, [wyib sl 1, k1] four times; rep from *, end k1.

Row 22 With A, p1, *p1, [wyif sl 1, k1] three times, wyif sl 1, p2; rep from * to end.

Row 23 With B, knit.

Row 24 With B, k1, *k1, p7, k3, p7, k2; rep from * to end.

Row 25 With A, *k3, [wyib sl 1, k1] three times, k1; rep from *, end k1.

Row 26 With A, p1, *p2, [wyif sl 1, k1] twice, wyif sl 1, p3; rep from * to end.

Row 27 With B, knit.

Row 28 With B, k1, *k2, p5, k5, p5, k3; rep from * to end.

Row 29 With A, *k4, wyib sl 1, k1, wyib sl 1, k3; rep from *, end k1.

Row 30 With A, p1, *p3, wyif sl 1, k1, wyif sl 1, p4; rep from * to end.

Row 31 With B, knit.

Row 32 With B, k1, *k3, p3, k7, p3, k4; rep from * to end.

Rep rows 1–32.

**Color Key**

A orange

B rust

**Stitch Key**

☐ K on RS, P on WS

⊟ P on RS, K on WS

▽ wyib sl 1 on RS, wyif sl 1 on WS

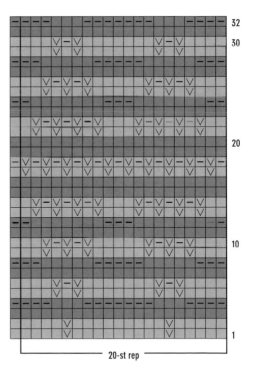

20-st rep

197

# 198 pie crust

(multiple of 10 sts)

Row 1 (RS) With A, knit.

Row 2 With A, purl.

Row 3 With B, *k3, wyib sl 2, k5; rep from * to end.

Row 4 With B, *p5, wyif sl 2, p3, rep from * to end.

Row 5 With A, *wyib sl 1, k1, wyib sl 1, k2; rep from * to end.

Row 6 With A, *p2, wyif sl 1, p1, wyif sl 1; rep from * to end.

Rows 7 and 11 With B, *k8, wyib sl 2; rep from * to end.

Rows 8 and 12 With B, *wyif sl 2, p8; rep from * to end.

Row 9 With A ,*wyib sl 1, k6, wyib sl 1, k2; rep from * to end.

Row 10 With A, *p2, wyif sl 1, p6, wyif sl 1; rep from * to end.

Row 13 With A, *wyib sl 1, k1, wyib sl 1, k2; rep from * to end.

Row 14 With A, *p2, wyif sl 1, p1, wyif sl 1; rep from * to end.

Row 15 With B, *k3, wyib sl 2, k5; rep from * to end.

Row 16 With B, *p5, wyif sl 2, p3; rep from * to end.

Row 17 With A, *[k2, wyib sl 1] twice, k4; rep from * to end.

Row 18 With A, *p4, [wyif sl 1, p2] twice; rep from * to end.

Rep rows 1–18.

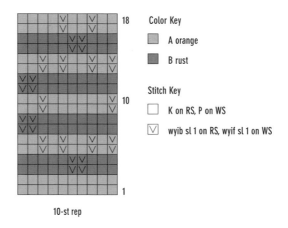

**Color Key**

A orange

B rust

**Stitch Key**

K on RS, P on WS

wyib sl 1 on RS, wyif sl 1 on WS

10-st rep

(multiple of 8 sts)

Row 1 (RS) With A, *k2, [wyib sl 1, k1] three times; rep from * to end.
Row 2 With A, *k1, [wyif sl 1, p1] twice, wyif sl 1, k2; rep from * to end.
Row 3 With B *k3, wyib sl 1, k1, wyib sl 1, k2; rep from * to end
Row 4 With B *k2, wyif sl 1, p1, wyif sl 1, k3; rep from * to end.
Row 5 With A, *k4, wyib sl 1, k3; rep from * to end.
Row 6 With A, *k1, p2, wyif sl 1, p3, k1; rep from * to end.
Row 7 With B, *k1, wyib sl 1, k6; rep from * to end.
Row 8 With B, *k3, p1, k2, wyif sl 1, k1; rep from * to end.
Row 9 With A, *k2, [wyib sl 1, k1] 3 times; rep from * to end.
Row 10 With A, *[k1, wyif sl 1] 3 times, p1, k1; rep from * to end.

Row 11 With B, *k1, wyib sl 1, k6; rep from * to end.
Row 12 With B, *k3, p1, k2, wyif sl 1, k1; rep from * to end.
Row 13 With A, *k4, wyib sl 1, k3; rep from * to end.
Row 14 With A, *k1, p2, wyif sl 1, p3, k1; rep from * to end.
Row 15 With B, *k3, wyib sl 1, k1, wyib sl 1, k2; rep from * to end.
Row 16 With B, *k2, wyif sl 1, p1, wyif sl 1, k3; rep from * to end.
Row 17 With A, *k2, [wyib sl 1, k1] three times; rep from * to end.
Row 18 With A, *k1, [wyif sl 1, k1] twice, wyif sl 1, k2; rep from * to end.
Rows 19 and 21 With B, knit.
Row 20 With B, knit.
Rows 22, 26, 30 and 34 With B, k1, p6, k1; rep from * to end.
Rows 23, 27 and 31 With A, *[k1, wyib sl 1] 3 times, k2; rep from * to end.
Rows 24, 28 and 32 With A, *k2, [wyif sl 1, k1] 3 times; rep from * to end.
Rows 25, 29 and 33 With B, knit.
Row 35 With B, *k1, p6, k1; rep from * to end.
Row 36 With B, *k1, p6, k1; rep from * to end.
Rep rows 1–36.

**Color Key**

☐ A light green

◼ B dark green

**Stitch Key**

☐ K on RS, P on WS

─ P on RS, K on WS

☑ wyib sl 1 on RS, wyif sl 1 on WS

8-st rep

(multiple of 16 sts plus 3)

Row 1 (RS) With B, k1, * k1, wyib sl 1, k3, wyib sl 1, k1, [wyib sl 1, k3] twice, wyib sl 1; rep from *, end k2.

Row 2 With B, p2, *[wyif sl 1, p3] twice, wyif sl 1, p1, wyif sl 1, p3, wyif sl 1, p1; rep from *, end p1.

Row 3 With A, k1, *wyib sl 1, k3; rep from *, end wyib sl 1, k1.

Row 4 With A, p1, wyif sl 1, *p3, wyif sl 1; rep from *, end p1.

Row 5 With B, k1, *k2, [k1, wyib sl 1] twice, [k3, wyib sl 1] twice, k2; rep from *, end k2.

Row 6 With B, p2, *p2, [wyif sl 1, p3] twice, wyif sl 1, p1, wyif sl 1, p3; rep from *, end p1.

Row 7 With A, k1, *k1, wyib sl 2, [k3, wyib sl 1] three times, wyib sl 1; rep from *, end k1, wyib sl 1.

Row 8 With A, wyif sl 1, p1, *wyif sl 2, [p3, wyif sl 1] three times, wyif sl 1, p1; rep from *, end p1.

Row 9 With B, k1, *[k3, wyib sl 1] 3 times, k1, wyib sl 1, k2; rep from *, end k2.

Row 10 With B, p2, *p2, wyif sl 1, p1, [wyif sl 1, p3] three times; rep from *, end p1.

Row 11 With A, k1, *wyib sl 1, k3; rep from *, end sl 1, k1.

Row 12 With A, p1, wyif sl 1, *p3, wyif sl 1; rep from *, end p1.

Row 13 With B, k1, *k1, [wyib sl 1, k3] twice, wyib sl 1, k1, wyib sl 1, k3, wyib sl 1; rep from *, end k2.

Row 14 With B, p2, *wyif sl 1, p3, wyif sl 1, p1, wyif sl 1, [p3, wyif sl 1] twice, p1; rep from *, end p1.

Row 15 With A, k1, *k2, wyib sl 1, k1; rep from *, end k2.

Row 16 With A, p2, *p1, wyif sl 1, p2; rep from *, end p1.

Row 17 With B, k1, * [k1, wyib sl 1] twice, k3, [wyib sl 1, k1] twice, k2, wyib sl 1, k2; rep from *, end k2.

Row 18 With B, p2, *p2, wyif sl 1, [p3, wyif sl 1, p1, wyif sl 1] twice, p1; rep from *, end p1.

Row 19 With A, k1, * wyib sl 1, k3; rep from *, end wyib sl 1, k1.

Row 20 With A, p1, wyif sl 1, *p3, wyif sl 1; rep from *, end p1.

Row 21 With B, k1, *k3, wyib sl 1, k1, wyib sl 1, k5, wyib sl 1, k3, wyib sl 1; rep from *, end k2.

Row 22 With B, p2, *[wyif sl 1, p3] twice, p2, [wyif sl 1, p1] twice, p2; rep from *, end p1.

Row 23 With A, k1, *k2, wyib sl 1, k3, wyib sl 2, k1, wyib sl 2, k3, wyib sl 1, k1; rep from *, end k2.

Row 24 With A, p2, *p1, wyif sl 1, p3, wyif sl 2, p1, wyif sl 2, p3, wyif sl 1, p2; rep from *, end p1.

Row 25 With B, k1, *k1, [wyib sl 1, k3] twice, k2, [wyib sl 1, k1] twice, k1; rep from *, end k2.

Row 26 With B, p2, *p2, wyif sl 1, p1, wyif sl 1, p5, wyif sl 1, p3, wyif sl 1, p1; rep from *, end p1.

Row 27 With A, k1, *wyib sl 1, k3; rep from *, end wyib sl 1, k1.

Row 28 With A, p1, wyif sl 1, *p3, wyif sl 1; rep from *, end p1.

Row 29 With B, k1, *[k3, wyib sl 1] twice, k1, wyib sl 1, k3, wyib sl 1, k1, wyib sl 1; rep from *, end k2.

Row 30 With B, p2, *[wyif sl 1, p1] twice, p2, wyif sl 1, p1, [wyif sl 1, p3] twice; rep from *, end p1.

Row 31 With A, k1, *k2, wyib sl 1, k1; rep from *, end k2.

Row 32 With A, p2, * p1, wyif sl 1, p2; rep from *, end p1.

Rep rows 1–32.

# 201 scooter pie

## Color Key

- ☐ A peach
- ■ B rust

## Stitch Key

- ☐ K on RS, P on WS
- ⊽ wyib sl 1 on RS, wyif sl 1 on WS

(multiple of 12 sts plus 2)

Rows 1, 5, 9 and 13 (RS) With MC, knit.

Rows 2, 6, 10 and 14 With MC, purl.

Rows 3 and 7 With A, *wyib sl 2, k10; rep from *, end wyib sl 2.

Rows 4 and 8 With A, wyif sl 2, *k10, wyif sl 2; rep from * to end.

Rows 11 and 15 With A, *k6, wyib sl 2, k4; rep from *, end k2.

Rows 12 and 16 With A, k2, *k4, wyif sl 2, k6; rep from * to end.

Rep rows 1–16.

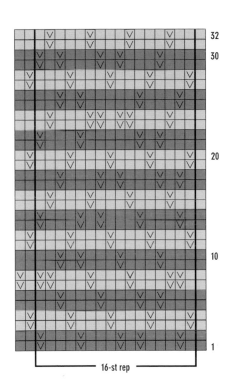

16-st rep

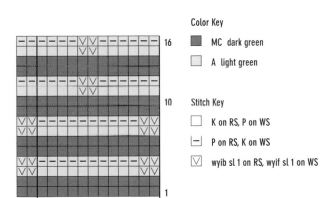

## Color Key

- ■ MC dark green
- ☐ A light green

## Stitch Key

- ☐ K on RS, P on WS
- ⊟ P on RS, K on WS
- ⊽ wyib sl 1 on RS, wyif sl 1 on WS

12-st rep

201

(multiple of 44 sts)

Rows 1, 5, 9, 13, 17 and 21 (RS) With A, *[wyib sl 1, k1] 5 times, k6, [wyib sl 1, k1] 5 times, k6, [wyib sl 1, k1] 3 times, k6; rep from * to end.

Rows 2, 6, 10, 14, 18 and 22 With A, *k6, [p1, wyif sl 1] 3 times, k6, [p1, wyif sl 1] 5 times, k6, [p1, wyif sl 1] 5 times; rep from * to end.

Rows 3, 7, 11, 15, 19 and 23 With B, *[k1, wyib sl 1] 5 times, k6, [k1, wyib sl 1] 5 times, k6, [k1, wyib sl 1] 3 times, k6; rep from * to end.

Rows 4, 8, 12, 16, 20 and 24 With B, *k6, [wyif sl 1, p1] 3 times, k6, [wyif sl 1, p1] 5 times, k6, [wyif sl 1, p1] 5 times; rep from * to end.

Rows 25 and 29 With A, *k10, [wyib sl 1, k1] 3 times, k10, [wyib sl 1, k1] 3 times, k6, [wyib sl 1, k1] 3 times; rep from * to end.

Row 26 and 30 With A, *[p1, wyif sl 1] 3 times, k6, [p1, wyif sl 1] 3 times, k10, [p1, wyif sl 1] 3 times, k10; rep from * to end.

Rows 27 and 31 With B, *k10, [k1, wyib sl 1] 3 times, k10, [k1, wyib sl 1] 3 times, k6, [k1, wyib sl 1] 3 times; rep from * to end.

Rows 28 and 32 With B, *[wyif sl 1, p1] 3 times, k6, [wyif sl 1, p1] 3 times, k10, [wyif sl 1, p1] 3 times, k10; rep from * to end.

Rows 33 and 37 With A, *[wyib sl 1, k1] 5 times, k6, [wyib sl 1, k1] 5 times, k6, [wyib sl 1, k1] 3 times, k6; rep from * to end.

Rows 34 and 38 With A, *k6, [p1, wyif sl 1] 3 times, k6, [p1, wyif sl 1] 5 times, k6, [p1, wyif sl 1] 5 times; rep from * to end.

Rows 35 and 39 With B, *[k1, wyib sl 1] 5 times, k6, [k1, wyib sl 1] 5 times, k6, [k1, wyib sl 1] 3 times, k6; rep from * to end.

Rows 36 and 40 With B, *k6, [wyif sl 1, p1] 3 times, k6, [wyif sl 1, p1] 5 times, k6, [wyif sl 1, p1] 5 times; rep from * to end.

Rows 41 and 45 With A, *k10, [wyib sl 1, k1] 3 times, k10, [wyib sl 1, k1] 3 times, k6, [wyib sl 1, k1] 3 times; rep from * to end.

Rows 42 and 46 With A, *[p1, wyif sl 1] 3 times, k6, [p1, wyif sl 1] 3 times, k10, [p1, wyif sl 1] 3 times, k10; rep from * to end.

Rows 43 and 47 With B, *k10, [k1, wyib sl 1] 3 times, k10, [k1, wyib sl 1] 3 times, k6, [k1, wyib sl 1] 3 times; rep from * to end.

Row 44 With B, *[wyif sl 1, p1] 3 times, k6, [wyif sl 1, p1] 3 times, k10, [wyif sl 1, p1] 3 times, k10; rep from * to end.

Row 48 With B, *[wyif sl 1, p1] 3 times, k6, [wyif sl 1, p1] 3 times, k10, [wyif sl 1, p1] 3 times, k10; rep from * to end.

Rep rows 1–48.

202

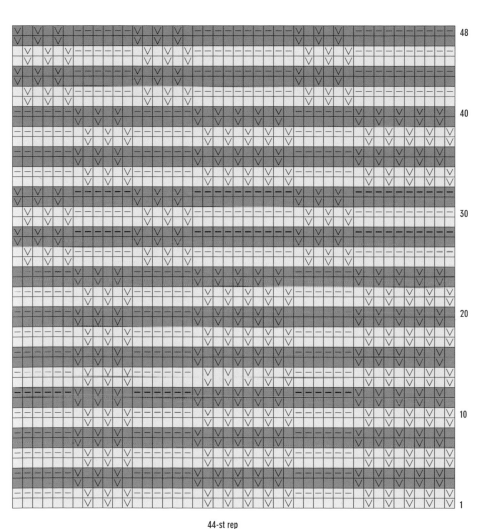

44-st rep

**Color Key**

⬜ A light green

🟩 B dark green

**Stitch Key**

⬜ K on RS, P on WS

— P on RS, K on WS

∨ wyib sl 1 on RS, wyif sl 1 on WS

(multiple of 6 sts plus 4)

Row 1 (RS) With MC, knit.

Row 2 With MC, purl.

Rows 3 and 19 With A, k4, *wyib sl 2, k4; rep from * to end.

Rows 4 and 20 With A, *p4, wyif sl 2; rep from *, end p4.

Rows 5 and 17 With MC, k3, wyib sl 1, *k2, wyib sl 1; rep from * to end.

Rows 6 and 18 With MC, *wyif sl 1, p2; rep from *, end wyif sl 1, p3.

Rows 7 and 15 With A, k1, wyib sl 2, k1, *k3, wyib sl 2, k1; rep from * to end.

Rows 8 and 16 With A, *p1, wyif sl 2, p3; rep from *, end p1, wyif sl 2, p1.

Rows 9, 13 and 21 With MC, knit.

Rows 10 and 14 With MC, purl.

Row 11 With B, *k1, wyib sl 1; rep from * to end.

Row 12 With B, *wyif sl 1, p1; rep from * to end.

Row 22 With MC, purl.

Rep rows 1–22.

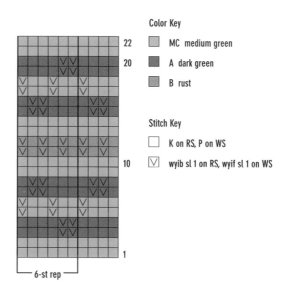

**Color Key**

MC medium green

A dark green

B rust

**Stitch Key**

K on RS, P on WS

wyib sl 1 on RS, wyif sl 1 on WS

6-st rep

# 204 succotash

(multiple of 4 sts)

**Note** Pattern is worked back and forth in rows on dpn or circular needle.

**Preparation row (WS)** With MC, purl.

**Row 1 (RS)** With A, *k2, sl 2 wyib; rep from * to end. Do not turn. Slide sts back to opposite end of needle.

**Row 2 (RS)** With MC, *wyib sl 2, k2; rep from * to end.

**Row 3 (WS)** With B, *wyif sl 2, p2; rep from * to end. Do not turn. Slide sts back to opposite end of needle.

**Row 4 (WS)** With MC, *p2, wyif sl 2; rep from * to end.

**Row 5 (RS)** With C, *wyib sl 2, k2; rep from * to end. Do not turn. Slide sts back to opposite end of needle.

**Row 6 (RS)** With MC, *k2, wyib sl 2; rep from * to end.

**Row 7 (WS)** With D, *p2, wyif sl 2; rep from * to end. Do not turn. Slide sts back to opposite end of needle.

**Row 8 (WS)** With MC, *wyif sl 2, p2; rep from * to end.

Rep rows 1–8.

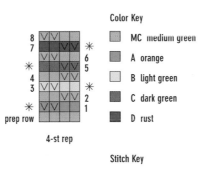

**Color Key**

| | |
|---|---|
| | MC medium green |
| | A orange |
| | B light green |
| | C dark green |
| | D rust |

4-st rep

**Stitch Key**

| | |
|---|---|
| ☐ | wyib sl 1 on RS, wyif sl 1 on WS |
| ✳ | slide sts back to opposite end of needle |

(multiple of 8 sts plus 1)

**Row 1 (RS)** With B, knit.

**Row 2** With B, knit.

**Row 3** With A, *k1, wyib sl 1; rep from *, end k1.

**Row 4** With A, p1, *wyif sl 1, p1; rep from * to end.

**Rows 5 and 6** With B, knit.

**Row 7** With A, *k1, wyib sl 1, k5, wyib sl 1; rep from *, end k1.

**Row 8** With A, k1, *wyif sl 1, k5, wyif sl 1, k1; rep from * to end.

**Rows 9 and 13** With B, *k2, wyib sl 1, k3, wyib sl 1, k1; rep from *, end k1.

**Rows 10 and 14** With B, k1, *k1, wyif sl 1, k3, wyif sl 1, k2; rep from * to end.

**Row 11** With A, *k1, wyib sl 1; rep from *, end k1.

**Row 12** With A, k1, *wyif sl 1, k1; rep from * to end.

**Row 15** With A, *k1, wyib sl 1, k5, wyib sl 1; rep from *, end k1.

**Row 16** With A, k1, *wyif sl 1, k5, wyif sl 1, k1; rep from * to end.

Rep rows 1–16.

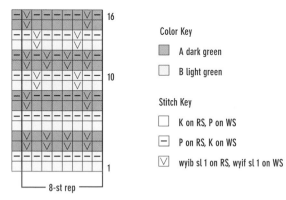

**Color Key**

⬜ A dark green

⬜ B light green

**Stitch Key**

☐ K on RS, P on WS

— P on RS, K on WS

⊻ wyib sl 1 on RS, wyif sl 1 on WS

8-st rep

# abbreviations

approx — approximately

beg — begin; begins; beginning

cn — cable needle

cont — continue; continuing

dec — decrease; decreasing

dpn — double-pointed needle

inc — increase; increasing

k — knit

k-b; k1-b — knit stitch in row below

k2tog — knit two together

k3tog — knit three together

LH — left hand

lp; lps — loop; loops

m1 — make one

m1 p-st — make one purl stitch

p — purl

pat; pats — pattern; patterns

pm — place marker

psso — pass slip stitch over

p2tog — purl two together

p3tog — purl three together

rem — remain; remaining

rep — repeat

RH — right-hand

RS — right side

SKP — slip one, knit one, pass slip stitch over

SK2P — slip one, knit two together, pass slip stitch over

sl — slip

sm — slip marker

ssk — slip, slip, knit

st; sts — stitch; stitches

St st — stockinette stitch

tbl — through back loop

tog — together

WS — wrong side

wyib — with yarn in back

wyif — with yarn in front

yo — yarn over

yo twice; yo2 — yarn over two times

yof — yarn over front

## Yarn overs

### 1. Between two knit stitches

Bring the yarn from the back of the work to the front between the two needles. Knit the next stitch, bringing the yarn to the back over the right needle as shown.

### 2. Between two purl stitches

Leave the yarn at the front of the work. Bring the yarn to the back over the right needle and to the front again as shown. Purl the next stitch.

### 3. Between a knit and a purl stitch

Bring the yarn from the back to the front between the two needles, then to the back over the right needle and to the front again as shown. Purl the next stitch.

### 4. Between a purl and a knit stitch

Leave the yarn at the front of the work. Knit the next stitch, bringing the yarn to the back over the right needle as shown.

### 5. At the beginning of a knit row

Keep the yarn at the front of the work. Insert the right needle knitwise into the first stitch on the left needle. Bring the yarn over the right needle to the back and knit the next stitch, holding the yarn over with your thumb if necessary.

### 6. At the beginning of a purl row

To work a yarn over at the beginning of a purl row, keep the yarn at the back of the work. Insert the right needle purlwise into the first stitch on the left needle. Purl the stitch.

### 7. Multiple yarn overs

a. For multiple yarn overs (two or more), wrap the yarn around the needle as for a single yarn over, then wrap the yarn around the needle once more (or as many times as indicated). Work the next stitch on the left needle.

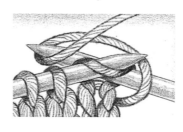

b. Alternate knitting and purling into the multiple yarn over on the subsequent row, always knitting the last stitch on a purl row and purling the last stitch on a knit row.

# glossary

**as foll** Work the instructions that follow.

**end last rep** After completing a full repeat of a pattern and not enough stitches remain to complete another repeat, end the pattern repeat as directed.

**hold to front (back) of work** A term usually referring to stitches placed on a cable needle that are held to the front (or the back) of the work as it faces you.

**k the knit sts and p the purl sts (as they face you)** A phrase used when a pattern of knit and purl stitches has been established and will continue for a determined length (such as ribbing). Work the stitches as they face you: Knit the knit stitches and purl the purl stitches.

**k the purl sts and p the knit sts:** A phrase used when a pattern of knit and purl stitches will alternate on the following row or rows (such as in a seed stitch pattern). Work the stitches opposite of how they face you: Purl the knit stitches and knit the purl stitches.

**knitwise (or as to knit)** Insert the needle into the stitch as if you were going to knit it.

**m1** Make one knit stitch as follows: Insert left needle from front to back under horizontal strand between stitch just worked and next stitch on left needle. Knit this strand through the back loop.

**m1 p-st** Make one purl stitch as follows: Insert left needle from front to back under horizontal strand between stitch just worked and next stitch on left needle. Purl this strand through the back loop.

**multiple of . . . sts** Used when working a pattern. The total number of stitches should be divisible by the number of stitches in one pattern repeat.

**multiple of . . . sts plus . . .** Used when working a pattern. The total number of stitches should be divisible by the number of stitches in one pattern repeat, plus the extra stitches (added only once).

**next row (RS), or (WS)** The row following the one just worked will be a right side (or wrong side) row.

**place marker(s)** Slide a stitch marker either onto the needle (where it is slipped every row) or attach it to a stitch, where it remains as a guide.

**preparation row** A row that sets up the stitch pattern but is not part of the pattern repeat.

**purlwise** Insert the needle into the stitch as if you were going to purl it.

**rep from *, end . . .** Repeat the instructions that begin at the asterisk as many times as you can work full repeats of the pattern, then end the row as directed.

**rep from * to end** Repeat the instructions that begin at the asterisk, ending the row with a full repeat of the pattern.

**rep . . . times more** Repeat a direction the designated number of times (not counting the first time you work it).

**right side (or RS)** Usually refers to the surface of the work that will face outside when the garment is worn.

**row 2 and all WS (even-numbered) rows** A term used when all the wrong-side or even-numbered rows are worked the same.

**skp** On RS, slip one stitch. Knit next stitch and pass slip stitch over knit stitch. On WS, slip next two stitches knitwise. Slip these two stitches back to left needle without twisting them and purl them together through the back loops.

**sk2p** On RS, slip one stitch, knit two stitches together. Pass slipped stitch over two stitches knit together. On WS, slip two stitches to right needle as if knitting two together. Slip next stitch knitwise. Slip all stitches to left needle without twisting them. Purl these three stitches together through back loops.

**slip marker** To keep the stitch marker in the same position from one row to the next, transfer it from one needle to the other as you work each row.

**ssk** On RS, slip next two stitches knitwise. Insert tip of left needle into fronts of these two stitches and knit them together. On WS, slip one stitch, purl one stitch, then pass slip stitch over purl stitch.

**stockinette stitch** Knit every right-side row and purl every wrong-side row.

**work to end** Work the established pattern to the end of the row.

# acknowledgments

Special thanks to:


The Knitters:

Jeannie Chin

Victoria Hilditch

Margarita Mejia

Charlotte Parry


And also:

Maria Gerbino

Tanis Gray

Claire Hilditch

Jenn Jarvis

Mary Kathryn Simon

Yarn provided by:

GGH Yarns

distributed by Muench Yarns


Jaeger Handknits

distributed by Westminster Fibers, Inc.


Lana Grossa

distributed by Unicorn Books & Crafts, Inc.


Muench Yarns

1323 Scott Street

Petaluma, CA 94954-1135

www.myyarn.com


Unicorn Books & Crafts

1338 Ross St.

Petaluma, CA 94954

www.unicornbooks.com


Westminster Fibers, Inc.

4 Townsend West, Unit 8

Nashua, NH 03063

www.westminsterfibers.com


Knitting needles on cover provided by Lantern Moon.

Lantern Moon knitting needles are currently available in 4 distinct wood varieties.

Made entirely by hand, they are the perfect tool for knitters. The design detail and handfinishing

makes these needles as wonderful to work with as they are beautiful. Visit Lantern Moon online at

www.lanternmoon.com.